HORSES TO FOLLOW

2018/19 JUMPS SEASON

CONTENTS

TIMEF⦿RM

Timeform Horses To Follow is published by Timeform Limited, Halifax, West Yorkshire HX1 1XF (Tel: 01422 330330; e-mail: timeform@timeform.com).

ISBN 978-1-9997783-2-3   Price £9.95

Printed and bound by
Charlesworth Press,
Wakefield, UK 01924 204830

SECTION

Timeform's Fifty To Follow, carefully chosen by members of Timeform's editorial staff, are listed below with their respective page numbers. A selection of ten (**marked in bold with a** ★) is made for those who prefer a smaller list.

The form summary for each horse is shown after its age, colour, sex and pedigree. The summary shows the distance, the state of the going and where the horse finished in each of its races since the start of the 2017/18 season. Performances are in chronological sequence with the date of its last race shown at the end (F–ran on Flat).

The distance of each race is given in furlongs. Steeplechase form figures are prefixed by the letter 'c', hurdle form figures by the letter 'h' and NH Flat race or bumper form figures by the letter 'b'.

The going is symbolised as follows: f–firm, m–good to firm; g–good, d–good to soft; s–soft; v–heavy.

Placings are indicated, up to the sixth place, by use of superior figures, an asterisk being used to denote a win and superior letters are used to convey what happened to a horse during the race: F–fell, pu–pulled up, ur–unseated rider, bd–brought down, su–slipped up, ro–ran out.

The Timeform Rating of a horse is simply the merit of the horse expressed in pounds and is arrived at by careful examination of its running against other horses. The ratings range from 175+ for the champions down to a figure of around 55 for selling platers. Symbols attached to the ratings: 'p'–likely to improve; 'P'–capable of much better form; '+'–the horse may be better than we have rated it.

Acting Lass (Ire)   c149p

7 b.g. King's Theatre (Ire) – Darrens Lass (Ire) (Montelimar (USA))
2017/18 c21.4d* c20.2s* c21v* c24g Feb 24

By King's Theatre and out of a 3m winner named Darrens Lass, you would think that Acting Lass was well-named, as well as stoutly-bred. That is, of course, until you realise that 'she' is actually a 'he'. Added to the list of commentators' least-favourite horses, as well as last season's *Fifty*, Acting Lass became an oft-heard name in the early stages of the campaign, recording a hat-trick in handicaps with more in hand than the official winning distances would suggest between November and January. He justified good support to make a successful start over fences at Market Rasen (on the quickest ground he had faced at that stage) and progressed further when again beating three rivals, this time at Leicester, seven weeks later. He conceded weight to all there, impressing most with his jumping having tanked his way into the lead before the fourth, but was ridden with more restraint when completing his hat-trick at Ascot just nine days later, finding plenty at the end of 21f to make a winning start outside of novice company over fences.

As a result, it was something of a surprise that Acting Lass failed to make any sort of impression when stepped up to 3m for the first time at Kempton in late-February, though there were mitigating factors on the day—his stable wasn't in the best of form at the time and his position towards the inside was far from the ideal place to be. That experience in a big field should at least stand him in good stead this season and he deserves another chance to build on the positive impression he created in his three prior starts over fences, with another try over 3m likely to be on the cards if his trainer's comments—'We've always thought that he'd make a 3m chaser'—are anything to go by. **Harry Fry**

Conclusion: *Lengthy gelding whose (slightly idle) style of racing means he could stay ahead of the handicapper this term; likely to stay 3m*

Aimee de Sivola (Fr)   b98

4 ch.f. Network (Ger) – Neva de Sivola (Fr) (Blushing Flame (USA))
2017/18 b14s⁴ b12.6s* b16.7v² b16v⁴ Mar 10

As far as we're aware, loyalty cards don't exist in horse racing breeding circles, something that Nick Williams may rue considering the association his yard has built with the Haras de Sivola stud in central France in recent years, one which most notably produced the top class hurdler Reve de Sivola.

The latest off the conveyor belt is Aimee de Sivola, who showed fairly useful form in all four of her bumper starts last term. After a promising debut at Warwick in November, it didn't take long for her fine attitude to catch the eye, responding well to open her account over 1½m at Newbury a month later, proving a stronger stayer than the runner-up when it came to the crunch. That performance prompted a rise in both class and trip, as she finished runner-up in a listed contest over 2m at Market Rasen in January. She kept on well when headed by Dissavril a furlong out—the pair pulling clear of the remainder—and again showed that stamina is her forte when a staying-on fourth in a similar contest at Sandown in March, where she might well have done better with more use made of her. Though the form of that race hasn't worked out that well so far, it has plenty of history, having been won by The Nipper and Cap Soleil in recent years (both multiple winners over hurdles the following season). **Nick Williams**

Conclusion: *Useful hurdling prospect this season, particularly when tackling further than 2m (half-sister to useful hurdler Urbain de Sivola, who stayed 2½m)*

Ballinslea Bridge (Ire)   h125p

6 b.g. Pierre – Feelin' Looser (Ire) (Mazaad)
2017/18 b16g² b16.4g² h20s² h16.7s² h18.6v* h19.3v* Feb 19

Olly Murphy has enjoyed a tremendous start to his training career and will be looking to build on his already notable success this season. One of his brigade who may have slipped under the radar slightly—and could gain him further recognition—is Ballinslea

Bridge. The six-year-old gelding has yet to run at a major festival, but don't be misled, as he's been sent off at no bigger than 7/2 on all six of his starts under Rules, suggesting he is held in pretty high regard.

After becoming a bit of a frustrating figure with plenty of seconds to his name, Ballinslea Bridge didn't need to improve to open his account in a novices' hurdle at Market Rasen in January. He then showcased further his talents when staying on strongly to defy a penalty at Carlisle the following month (form worked out nicely), well positioned throughout and nicely on top at the end, the stiffer track unsurprisingly suiting this winning Irish pointer.

Although quite keen during his races, if Ballinslea Bridge learns to settle better there's no reason why he can't progress again this spring, with well-contested, big-field handicaps likely to bring out the best in him. There could be a nice prize in him over fences in time, though he may be best kept to right-handed tracks in the short term (both wins going that way round and jumped right at Fakenham on his hurdling debut). *Olly Murphy*

Conclusion: *Looks the type to improve further over hurdles this season, sure to be suited by 2½m+*

Beakstown (Ire)   b95p
5 b.g. Stowaway – Midnight Reel (Ire) (Accordion)
2017/18 b16s² Feb 9

Dan Skelton sent out more winners in Britain (156) than any other jumps trainer in 2017/18, quite a feat given that it was just his fifth season with a licence. Clearly, quantity is not a problem at Skelton's state-of-the-art base in Warwickshire, but the one thing that he has perhaps missed is a proper Grade 1 horse to take him to all the big days, and for a man who has made it his stated ambition to become champion trainer, the emphasis will surely be on improving the quality of his string in the years ahead.

The first step will be getting that elusive first win at the highest level on the board, and there is no shortage of likely candidates for Skelton to go to war with this season, with Beakstown, in particular, appealing as a novice hurdler to follow. A winner of his sole start between the flags in Ireland, Beakstown stood out in the paddock ahead of his debut for Skelton in a bumper at Kempton in February and was very well backed to boot, going off the 100/30 favourite in a field chock-full of interesting newcomers. Though beaten five lengths into second by Commanche Red, one of the few who had the benefit of a previous run, Beakstown still made a most encouraging start to his career under Rules, travelling as well as any when hitting the front in the back straight, before being joined over three furlongs out and left behind by the winner late on. He certainly showed enough to suggest he is up to winning a similar event—an option in the opening weeks of the campaign—but it is over hurdles, and eventually fences, that his future lies, and it would be no surprise if there were some good races to be won with him in the novice hurdling division this season. **Dan Skelton**

Conclusion: *Scopey type who shaped very well on his sole start in bumpers and looks an exciting hurdling recruit; should stay further than 2m, but clearly isn't short of speed*

Benatar (Ire) ★   c150p
6 b.g. Beneficial – Carrigeen Lily (Ire) (Supreme Leader)
2017/18 c18.8g* c19.7s* c21d* c19.9s³ Mar 15

'We are strong/No one can tell us we're wrong.' So sang Pat Benatar in the eighties, and it would be no surprise if Gary Moore hummed a similar tune as he plotted a brave start to Benatar's chasing career in 2017/18. Considered good enough to contest the Mersey Novices' Hurdle at Aintree on his final start of the previous season, when finishing a very creditable fourth to Finian's Oscar, Benatar was pitched straight into handicap company for his debut over fences at Ascot in November and vindicated his trainer's boldness in some style, smothering a classy and competitive field with a blistering late surge.

Benatar (right) and Finian's Oscar jump the last together at Ascot

Perhaps with one eye on the bonus for winning races at both Plumpton and the Cheltenham Festival, Benatar was turned out just 16 days later, making no mistake as the odds-on favourite in a three-runner race at the East Sussex venue. Stepped up in grade for his next start in the Noel Novices' Chase at Ascot a month later, Benatar improved again to maintain his unbeaten record over fences, more comfortable back under patient tactics and finding plenty to hold off the late challenge of his old rival Finian's Oscar, who was conceding him 5 lb.

Benatar was kept fresh for his final start in the JLT Novices' Chase at the Cheltenham Festival, where he did well under the circumstances to finish third to Shattered Love, especially given that he raced very freely and returned lame after suffering a pelvis injury. While it's a bit unnerving to include a horse in the *Fifty* who was injured when last seen, encouragement can be taken from the fact that Moore suggested Benatar could have run at Sandown on the final day of the season. It's more likely that connections merely decided to draw stumps with an eye on the big Grade 1 chases this season, and while he's not short of speed, the former point-to-point winner is bred to stay well, which certainly opens up plenty of options, one of which could be the Ascot Chase in February. ***Gary Moore***

Conclusion: *Already much better over fences than hurdles and looks the type to take another step forward this season; current quotes of 40/1 for the Ryanair Chase look tempting*

Black Op (Ire) ★   h152

7 br.g. Sandmason – Afar Story (Ire) (Desert Story (Ire))
2017/18 h16.3d⁴ h20.8s* h20.3v² h21.1s² h20s* Apr 14

Black Op earned a place in last year's *Fifty* as a novice hurdler to follow having shown plenty in bumpers in 2016/17, and he fully justified his inclusion, winning two of his five starts. He made a promising start to his hurdling career over an inadequate 2m at Newbury in December, and quickly left that form well behind when a flawless winner of a maiden hurdle over 2½m at Doncaster on his next start, scoring by 17 lengths. Black Op wasn't disgraced when beaten three quarters of a length into second by Santini in the Classic Novices' Hurdle at Cheltenham next time, and shaped even better when filling the same position in the Ballymore Novices' Hurdle at the Festival in March, beaten two and three quarter lengths by Samcro. He didn't have those two rivals in opposition when gaining his first Grade 1 win in the Mersey Novices' Hurdle at Aintree the following month, but his sloppy jumping nearly proved costly, and it was his game attitude that pulled the iron from the fire in the final 50 yards. A tall, good-topped gelding, Black Op is very much a chaser on looks, and is hopefully the clichéd type to treat fences with more respect. ***Tom George***

Conclusion: *Grade 1-winning novice hurdler who has a raft of solid form to his name and looks the type to prove at least as good over fences this season; an exciting prospect for novice chases*

Black Pirate   b107

6 b.g. Black Sam Bellamy (Ire) – Proper Posh (Rakaposhi King)
2017/18 b16v* b16v* b16g² Apr 21

The Black Pirate was a 1926 silent adventure film starring the legendary Douglas Fairbanks, who plays a young man seeking revenge on the pirate band responsible for his father's death; Fairbanks' character ultimately gets his happy ending, leading a successful assault on the pirates and marrying the girl whom they had been holding as captive. The equine Black Pirate also lost his father recently, though not through acts of piracy—Black Sam Bellamy died in July, sadly, due to a heart problem—and the hope is that following James Ewart's charge this season will have a similarly happy outcome, with plenty of treasure waiting to be plundered in the months ahead.

Bought by Ewart for £75,000 as a five-year-old after impressively winning his sole outing in points, Black Pirate was gambled on (9/2 from 7/1) for his Rules debut in a bumper at Wetherby in February and looked a good prospect as he made a winning start, staying on strongly to win by eight lengths. He didn't have to improve on that form to follow up in a conditionals/amateur event at Ayr later that month, not out of second gear to defy a penalty, but it is his second back at that venue in April that makes him so interesting for the season ahead. In a bumper that has been won by the likes of Sprinter Sacre in recent years, Black Pirate ran a smashing race under a double penalty, beating all bar a really promising one to whom he was conceding 15 lb, beaten just three and a half lengths. That effort proved he is not ground dependent (both his previous wins came on heavy), and he rates a really good jumping prospect for his relatively small yard to go to war with this season. *James Ewart*

Conclusion: *Useful bumper performer who has a touch of class about him and is one to look forward to this season, likely to prove well suited by 2½m+ over jumps*

Braqueur d'Or (Fr)   c139

7 b.g. Epalo (Ger) – Hot d'Or (Fr) (Shafoun (Fr))
2017/18 h21g³ c25.8m² c22.6g* c21m* c20s³ c22.6m² h21.6d² c23.8m* c23.8g³ c26g⁴ c24d² c24.1g Apr 21

The chief aim of the *Fifty* is to identify winners for the core jumps season—the start of which coincides with the Charlie Hall meeting at Wetherby in early-November for many people—disregarding the fact that the campaign actually got underway just seven days after the last one ended at Sandown in April. Some trainers are more active than others during the summer months and Paul Nicholls is one who seems to have made a concerted effort to be quicker off the mark in more recent times—the 27 winners he saddled between May and September, in both 2016/17 and 2017/18, was a much-improved tally compared to previous years.

Braqueur d'Or was one of Nicholls' busiest horses during the summer of 2017, with eight starts already to his name when Bristol de Mai and co were limbering up for their seasonal debuts in the Charlie Hall. Those outings resulted in three wins as he immediately showed an upturn in form for the switch to fences, namely a pair of novice handicaps at Stratford/Newton Abbot in July and a handicap at Ludlow in October, and a BHA mark of 138 gave connections the chance to try their hand in better company as the jumps season proper began. Braqueur d'Or was not disgraced, either, when third in the Sodexo Gold Cup at Ascot and fourth in the Ladbrokes Trophy at Newbury, the joint-youngest in the field on the latter occasion and faring best of those that raced close to the pace. Last seen finishing down the field in a novice handicap at Ayr in April, when looking rusty after four months off, he can resume this season from a BHA mark of 135. That gives him plenty of options, eligible to run in races at a slightly lower level than those he contested last winter, and still only seven, there should be more races to be won with him. *Paul Nicholls*

Conclusion: *Acquitted himself well in the face of some stiff tasks last season and returns on a good mark, 4 lb lower than when fourth in the Ladbrokes Trophy; likely to prove best at shorter than 3¼m*

Brewin'Upastorm (Ire) ★   b112p

5 b.g. Milan – Daraheen Diamond (Ire) (Husyan (USA))
2017/18 b16.2s* b16.3v⁴ Feb 10

Few jumps trainers have made as big an impact in their first campaign as Olly Murphy did in 2017/18, with 47 winners and over £380,000 in prize money to his name. He certainly made a better fist of his first domestic campaign than long-time mentor Gordon Elliott managed in his native Ireland—Elliott recorded his first winner under Rules courtesy of Arresting at Perth in June 2006, but had still to record a winner in Ireland when Silver Birch won the Grand National the following year!

Murphy will be hoping to build on his positive start in the months ahead and Brewin'Upastorm could be the horse to help him do just that. A winner of his sole outing between the flags in Ireland, Brewin'Upastorm fetched £250,000 at the sales four days later—he was bought by Dan Skelton but moved by owner Barbara Hester without making an appearance for him—and made the perfect start to his career under Rules when impressively winning a conditionals/amateur bumper at Hereford in January, forging clear to win by nine lengths from subsequent Aintree Grade 2 bumper winner Portrush Ted. Stepped up in grade for a listed bumper at Newbury the following month, he again shaped well, for all that he lost his unbeaten record in fourth, possibly paying the price for a big move into contention entering the straight (lost two places in the final furlong). The involvement in a race of that nature will not have been lost of him, and described by Murphy as 'the best horse I've got in the yard' after his debut success, big things are expected of Brewin'Upastorm as a novice hurdler this season. *Olly Murphy*

Conclusion: *Showed why he has such a tall home reputation in two starts in bumpers last season and should have even more to offer as a novice hurdler; exciting prospect*

Cadeyrn (Ire) h126

6 b.g. Flemensfirth (USA) – Kapricia Speed (Fr) (Vertical Speed (Fr))
2017/18 h20d h19.5v⁴ h22v* h22s² h23.3v* Mar 17

Michael Scudamore has had some big days in his relatively brief training career to date, but he is unlikely to have enjoyed a sweeter 24 hours than those he experienced towards the end of February 2017. Having won the Devon National with Kingswell Theatre, Scudamore headed north the following day to Newcastle, all of 377 miles from Exeter, and proceeded to land the Eider Chase with Mysteree, leaving the trainer understandably ecstatic—'If Carlsberg did weekends, I think it would be very close to the one we have just had here at Eccleswall Court,' he wrote in his blog.

Kingswell Theatre and Mysteree are owned by John Murray and Lynne MacLennan, respectively, and that pair could have another interesting prospect for staying chases on their hands this season in the shape of Cadeyrn, whom they own in partnership. A winner of his sole outing in points, Cadeyrn shaped very much like a stayer in his three starts in bumpers in 2016/17, winning the second of them at Chepstow, and progressed from his first two starts over hurdles to open his account at Newcastle in January, when value for extra after looking like winning comfortably until dossing late on (won by a neck). Scudamore said after that success that 'the future for Cadeyrn is very exciting—I can't wait to see him over a fence next season', and the gelding was not overfaced in two subsequent starts last season, finishing second under a penalty back at Newcastle in February, before resuming winning ways on Midlands Grand National day at Uttoxeter, appearing to relish the step up to 23f. Likely to stay even further than that in time, it is easy to see why Scudamore harbours such high hopes for him over fences—he is every inch a chaser on looks—and there could be a big staying handicap on his agenda in the spring if he progresses as expected in the first half of the season. *Michael Scudamore*

Conclusion: *Strong, lengthy type who had a good first season over obstacles and should be at least as effective when going over fences in the coming months*

Dan Barber (Cadeyrn): *"Cadeyrn is unlikely to prove the best member of the Fifty in terms of ability, but nothing will be able to match him for looks, one of the most impressive physical specimens seen on Timeform's travels to the track last season. As his build might suggest, it's chasing that will prove Cadeyrn's calling, yet a 'warm-up' novice hurdle campaign still provided a pair of heavy-ground wins when ridden to sensibly make use of his strong-galloping nature, a characteristic that ought to prove even more potent with his attentions turned to fences."*

Captain Cattistock   h135

5 b.g. Black Sam Bellamy (Ire) – Pearl Buttons (Alflora (Ire))
2017/18 h19.5d⁴ h21.4s* h19.8v* h19.3s⁴ h21.4v* h20.3g⁴ Apr 18

Based just 20 minutes away in Ditcheat, Paul Nicholls is no stranger to success at Wincanton—he has saddled more winners at his local track than anywhere else since setting up shop at Manor Farm Stables in October 1991—but the 2016/17 campaign was remarkable even by his own very high standards. In a season when he recorded a career-best tally of 171 winners, Nicholls was successful with 50% of his runners at Wincanton (28/56), with the highlight coming courtesy of Frodon in the Grade 2 Rising Stars Novices' Chase, a race Nicholls has won ten times overall.

Nicholls was again crowned the leading trainer at Wincanton in the latest season with 16 winners, though he only had two to spare over nearest pursuer Colin Tizzard, and it could all have been very different but for Captain Cattistock. Fourth on his hurdling debut at Chepstow in October, Captain Cattistock went on to win three times at Wincanton, namely novice hurdles in November/March and a handicap in February. He ran at least as well in defeat when four and a quarter lengths fourth to Diese des Bieffes on his final start at Cheltenham in April, where he was arguably unlucky not to finish closer, likely to have given the winner plenty to think about but for making a total mess of the final flight. There is certainly a feeling that we didn't see the very best of Captain Cattistock last season, and as a winner of his sole outing in points, there should be plenty more to come from him as a novice chaser this time round; it would be no surprise if he ended up as Nicholls' horse for the Rising Stars given his fine record at the track. *Paul Nicholls*

Conclusion: *Point winner who was not overfaced in winning three of his six starts as a novice hurdler and has the physique to make an even better chaser; likely to prove well suited by 3m*

Claimantakinforgan (Fr) h147

6 b.g. Great Pretender (Ire) – Taquine d'Estrees (Fr) (Take Risks (Fr))
2017/18 h16.3d* h15.7d* h15.6s³ h16.4s⁵ h16g² Apr 21

The official Twitter account of owners Mike Grech and Stuart Parkin (@GrechParkin) has quickly established itself as one of the most informative in racing, with the feed featuring regular updates on the horses that they own. Their followers—amounting to over 3,500 at the time of writing—are also encouraged to share their thoughts as to how the Grech and Parkin horses should be campaigned, and the discussion regarding whether Claimantakinforgan should remain over hurdles or go over fences this season was one of the most hotly-contested, with a wide variety of races, ranging from the Arkle to the Stayers' Hurdle, being suggested as potential targets.

A consensus seems to have been reached eventually, however, with the account confirming during the summer that novice chasing is the plan, and Claimantakinforgan will be one to look out for in that division if replicating the smart form he showed over hurdles last season. Having justified odds-on favouritism on his debut at Newbury in November, he took the step up in grade in his stride to land the Kennel Gate Novices' Hurdle at Ascot the following month and went on to better that form in defeat in two of his three subsequent starts, namely when fifth in the Supreme Novices' Hurdle at Cheltenham (beaten five and a quarter lengths by Summerville Boy) and when second in the Scottish Champion Hurdle at Ayr (beaten just one and a quarter lengths from a BHA mark of 147). It was slightly surprising that he was campaigned solely over 2m last term—he was included in last year's *Fifty* as a horse who should have 'plenty more to offer' when going beyond that trip and often shaped as if that would be the case—but the plus side is that he remains with potential with longer trips still to explore; the JLT at Cheltenham appeals as a suitable target if he progresses as expected over fences. ***Nicky Henderson***

Conclusion: *Good-topped gelding who enjoyed a productive novice season over hurdles and looks the type to do even better as a chaser, especially when going up in trip*

Cyrname (Fr) c156

6 b.g. Nickname (Fr) – Narquille (Fr) (Passing Sale (Fr))
2017/18 h16d c16.5g* c16.4g² c16s* c20s² c20.5g* c19.9s⁴ Apr 12

Sean Bowen announced his arrival on the big stage with a power-packed ride to win the bet365 Gold Cup at Sandown in 2015, lifting the Paul Nicholls-trained Just A Par to victory in a manner reminiscent of AP McCoy. Bowen has been a permanent fixture at Ditcheat ever since, though opportunities were harder to come by in the latest

Cyrname was a very smart novice chaser last season

season—Sam Twiston-Davies, Harry Cobden and Bryony Frost all had more rides (and winners) for the yard than Bowen—and it was no great surprise that he was overlooked for the role as Nicholls' stable jockey in favour of Cobden, following the news in the spring that Twiston-Davies is to go freelance this season.

Nevertheless, Bowen still enjoyed the best season of his riding career so far in 2017/18, with 82 winners and over £1m in prize money for the first time, and his association with the very smart novice chaser Cyrname will almost certainly have been the highlight. Having failed to win in three starts over hurdles in 2016/17, Cyrname proved a completely different proposition as he made a successful chasing debut in a novice handicap at Huntingdon in November, winning by 14 lengths from a BHA mark of 130, and bounced back from a blip at Newbury—when jumping persistently right—to win the Wayward Lad Novices' Chase at Kempton over Christmas. Better was to come when stepped up in trip for his next two starts, when second to another member of the *Fifty*, Terrefort, in the Scilly Isles Novices' Chase at Sandown and winning the Pendil Novices' Chase back at Kempton, both in February, while his below-par effort on his final start at Aintree is best forgiven under the circumstances (went off too hard). On the face of things, he won't be all that easy to place this season with a BHA mark of 150 and his tendency to jump right, but Nicholls has few peers when it comes to finding opportunities for chasers just below the top drawer, and there are still enough good races to be won at around 2½m—going right-handed, of course—to justify his inclusion in this year's *Fifty*. **Paul Nicholls**

Conclusion: *Lots to like about his novice chasing campaign, with his only defeat when going right-handed over fences coming at the hands of the exciting Terrefort; could have more to offer this season and looks tailor-made for races such as the 1965 Chase at Ascot and the Peterborough Chase at Huntingdon*

Danny Kirwan (Ire) ★   b103P

5 b.g. Scorpion (Ire) – Sainte Baronne (Fr) (Saint des Saints (Fr))
2017/18 b16g* b17s Apr 13

Danny Kirwan will hopefully not be the albatross around the neck of this year's *Fifty*, the horse named not after the former Fleetwood Mac guitarist, but after a man from the town of Kilmacthomas in County Waterford, who celebrated his 100th birthday in 2016. Judging by the horse's performance on his Rules debut at Kempton last season, as well as his point win the previous October, that's unlikely to be the case. Described by Pat Doyle—who has moved on the likes of First Lieutenant, Shattered Love, Death Duty, Bacardys, Brindisi Breeze and No More Heroes—as `potentially the best horse I've ever trained in this age group' following his win at Lisronagh, Danny Kirwan was bought by Tom Malone for Mrs Johnny de la Hey. Danny Kirwan's winning bumper debut was actually a belated one, the horse having been declared a non-runner at Newbury a fortnight earlier due to soft going. His reputation preceded him at Kempton (sent off the well-backed 13/8 favourite) and he duly justified the hype, making headway on the bridle three furlongs out, despite taking a wider route, and just pushed out to score by two lengths.

Danny Kirwan was quickly pitched in at the deep end in the Grade 2 bumper at Aintree on his next start seven weeks later, but failed to run any sort of race despite being sent off the 11/4 favourite. He clearly wasn't 100% on the day, struggling over three furlongs out and unable to land a blow, though not persevered with once held. It might be that something was amiss or just that he didn't handle the soft ground, but whatever the reason he remains an exciting prospect, one who has `done plenty of jumping at home' according to his trainer. **Paul Nicholls**

Conclusion: *Runaway point winner who flopped at Aintree but is much better judged on his debut at Kempton where he created a huge impression; good ground likely to be key to his chances*

Dell Oro (Fr)   h133

5 b.g. Walk In The Park (Ire) – Kallistea (Fr) (Sicyos (USA))
2017/18 h15.7g* h16.3v² h19.6s⁴ h20.3g³ h21m² Apr 26

The stock of Derby runner-up Walk In The Park—whose sole win from 15 starts came in a minor event at Saint-Cloud—took a significant upturn in 2015, when Douvan and Min started to make their impact on the British and Irish jumps scene. The likes of Vado Forte (Tom Lacey), Walk In The Mill (Robert Walford) and Koshari (Willie Mullins) have all pitched in at a lower level since, along with the Gary Moore-trained Antony, a five-time winner who has secured three of those victories at Fontwell. The West Sussex venue was also the scene of his stablemate (and fellow Walk In The Park offspring) Dell Oro's debut win in March 2017, though it's his novice hurdling campaign of last term which makes him of most interest for the season ahead.

After winning a race previously won by Altior and My Tent Or Yours at Ascot on his reappearance in November, Dell Oro's progress stalled in two starts on soft going, before being reignited when third to Diese des Bieffes on good ground at Cheltenham in April, a run which confirmed his stamina for 2½m and was backed up by a good timefigure. Dell Oro was quickly turned out at Kempton just eight days later and really should have won, going like the best horse at the weights only to give it away when making a mistake at the last and idling, ultimately losing out by half a length to Who's My Jockey. The winner has since run well from a BHA mark of 136 and Dell Oro, who is a chaser on looks, is one to back on his first start in handicap company over fences—'I can't wait until we go chasing with him,' said his trainer Gary Moore last season—worth bearing in mind the success that his trainer had with Benatar in a similar situation last term. *Gary Moore*

Conclusion: *Won on reappearance for past two seasons and first-time-out likely to be the best time to catch him again; BHA mark of 136 looks workable with more improvement to come when sent chasing*

Diable de Sivola (Fr)   c129+

5 b.g. Noroit (Ger) – Grande Route (Ire) (Lost World (Ire))
2017/18 h19.2g² h21.1s⁴ h20.5vᶠ h16s³ h20.3g: 2018/19 c16d⁴ c20s⁵ c21.4m³ Jun 22

Included in last year's *Fifty* on the back of finishing fifth in the Fred Winter at the 2017 Cheltenham Festival, Diable de Sivola might not be the most obvious candidate for a repeat entry considering he has failed to add to his tally in eight subsequent starts. However, he was continually not seen to best effect over hurdles and that trend continued in three outings once switched to fences in early-summer. Very much a chaser on looks and breeding (half-brother to 17f chase winner in France, Cougar de

Sivola), Diable de Sivola was given a considerate introduction over an inadequate trip at Uttoxeter in May, catching the eye, and paid the price for some early jumping errors when fifth at Worcester later that month. He duly got back on track, and arguably wasn't seen to best effect, when third at Market Rasen last time. Waited with, he was not always fluent at his fences, but kept on well in the latter stages and was nearest at the finish after being set a lot to do off what was a messy gallop.

That run hasn't gone unnoticed by the BHA handicapper, who has nudged Diable de Sivola back up by 1 lb after dropping him previously, but he is still on a lower mark than when finishing fifth in the Fred Winter and the five-year-old is expected to reach greater heights over fences this season. **Nick Williams**

Conclusion: *Well-handicapped on peak hurdles form; acts on any ground and should have more to offer over fences*

Didtheyleaveuoutto (Ire)   b111+
5 ch.g. Presenting – Pretty Puttens (Ire) (Snurge)
2017/18 ab16g* b15.7d* b16.4s Mar 14

Pretty Puttens never made it to the racecourse, but her half-brother Denman certainly did; he won 14 races under Rules, with his huge stride and copper-bottomed stamina perhaps the key to his most prestigious success in the 2008 Cheltenham Gold Cup. Pretty Puttens' son Didtheyleaveuoutto, by Denman's sire Presenting, on the other hand, is a speedier type judged by his winning debut in an all-weather bumper at Lingfield in November—he covered the final two furlongs faster than all bar one Flat horse over the same C&D in 2017—but he also possesses a huge stride, and it would be no surprise to see the family's stamina manifest itself more when he goes over hurdles this season.

Didtheyleaveuoutto took on nine other previous winners for his second start in a listed event at Ascot in December and again showed a smart turn of foot off a slow pace, making smooth headway approaching the straight, quickening to lead over a furlong out and going on to win readily by two and three quarter lengths from the useful Bullionaire. Considered a good-ground horse by connections, Didtheyleaveuoutto was kept fresh and sent straight to the Champion Bumper for his next start nearly three months later, but found the soft going against him, alongside the winner Relegate early in the straight but unable to finish to anything like the same effect in mid-division.

Trainer Nick Gifford spoke about possibly going hurdling with Didtheyleaveuoutto immediately after his debut win, so expect to see him out early for experience before potentially being put away for a spring campaign on better ground. `The way he gallops at home he'll definitely want a trip,' said Gifford, and given the horse's stamina-laden pedigree, his future may lie in races such as the Ballymore Novices' Hurdle at the Cheltenham Festival rather than the shorter Supreme. **Nick Gifford**

Conclusion: *Exciting prospect who should make up into a genuine Grade 1 novice hurdler this season; has good turn of foot but may not see the best of him until stepped up to 2½m or further*

Dingo Dollar (Ire) c147p

6 ch.g. Golden Lariat (USA) – Social Society (Ire) (Moscow Society (USA))
2017/18 c23.6g⁴ c24.2sᶠ c23.4s* c24d* c24.1g² Apr 21

According to the stud's website, in what is a good impression of a Carlsberg advert, Golden Lariat is `probably the best looking Thoroughbred stallion that ever stood at Tullaghansleek Stud'. As we all know, looks aren't everything—it's what's inside that counts—but it appears that there is plenty of substance to Golden Lariat's offspring, too. Though far from prolific, he has sired the useful handicap chasers Fayette County and Pinch of Ginger, while Dingo Dollar is already the most successful of his offspring and easily the most exciting.

Picked up for £50,000 as a four-year-old after winning a point-to-point at Belharbour in a fast time, Dingo Dollar failed to flourish over hurdles, but he progressed well after being sent over fences last season, showing improved form to get off the mark in a handicap at Newbury in December and not needing to better that effort when following up in a three-runner novice event at Doncaster in February. Though Dingo Dollar met with defeat after 10 weeks off at Ayr in April, that represented another step forward in form terms, close to completing the hat-trick back in a handicap and doing especially well given that he was responsible for much of the strong pace, only beaten by an equally progressive sort in Crosshue Boy.

Valuable staying handicaps are on the agenda this season, with an early date in the Ladbrokes Trophy (formerly the Hennessy) at Newbury the likely first port of call in a campaign that has the Scottish National as a long-term target. **Alan King**

Conclusion: *Young staying chaser whose jumping improved as the campaign went on last season; has all the attributes to provide his trainer with a second win in the Scottish National*

Et Moi Alors (Fr) h117

4 b.g. Kap Rock (Fr) – Qui L'Eut Cru (Fr) (Lavirco (Ger))
2017/18 h15.7vᶠ h16v² h17s⁶ Apr 12

Et Moi Alors is trained by Gary Moore and owned by Ashley Head. So what (or et alors), you might say? Well, it means that the horse is likely to feature in the winners' enclosure at least once this season, the owner/trainer combination having already teamed up for 19 winners from 103 runners at the time of writing, to a level stakes profit of +£85.45.

Despite having no background in points, Et Moi Alors took the unconventional route of bypassing bumper races last season, instead making his first start under Rules in a novices' hurdle at Ascot in January where, despite his inexperience, he made a lasting impression, looking set to win before crashing out at the last when two lengths ahead. That form worked out reasonably well, with two of the three finishers going on to win subsequently, and Et Moi Alors was sent off heavily odds-on for his next start at Sandown. He failed to meet expectations, finishing second while still looking rough around the edges, and it's possible that the Ascot fall had left its mark. Connections were undeterred by his defeat, though, stepping him up into Grade 1 company at Aintree following a 55-day break. Whilst Et Moi Alors was a well-beaten sixth behind We Have A Dream that day, he showed that he still remains with potential, particularly if improving his jumping technique. Those three runs have now qualified Et Moi Alors for a mark, and it would be no surprise should he take off in handicaps this season. **Gary Moore**

Conclusion: *Showed plenty of promise in three starts and, assuming his jumping has been worked upon, he looks one to follow in handicaps this term*

Euxton Lane (Ire) h128

6 b.g. Getaway (Ger) – Local Hall (Ire) (Saddlers' Hall (Ire))
2017/18 h16.3d⁴ h20.8s* h20.3v² h21.1s² h20s* Apr 14

Named after a road that runs through Chorley in Lancashire, near to where his owner Trevor Hemmings' Gleadhill House Stud is situated, Euxton Lane made a most promising start to his career last season. Bred to excel over further, he shaped encouragingly when third on his debut in a bumper at Bangor in October and, as expected, was brought along slowly over hurdles thereafter, progressing in each of his runs before opening his account at the fourth attempt in a 2¼m maiden hurdle at Fontwell in March, winning by 17 lengths from a subsequent winner. His form prior to that win was strong, too, and he improved further to follow up under a penalty in a novice hurdle at Newbury (by three lengths) later that month, hitting the front two out and keeping on well to win by three lengths. Euxton Lane ran as well as could be expected on his final start, finishing mid-field in the Mersey Novices' Hurdle at Aintree, beaten eleven and a half lengths by another member of the *Fifty*, Black Op. Hemmings is known for buying strong, chasing types and Euxton Lane is very much the type to come into his own over fences this season, with the potential to make up into a smart novice chaser. **Oliver Sherwood**

Conclusion: *Strong gelding who progressed with every run over hurdles and looks the type to do even better over fences; likely to stay further than 2½m*

Global Citizen on his way to victory in the Dovecote Novices' Hurdle

Global Citizen (Ire) h142

6 b.g. Alkaadhem – Lady Willmurt (Ire) (Mandalus)
2017/18 b16f* h20d⁵ h15.8d² h15.7v* h16g* h16.5s⁶ Apr 13

Global Citizen won his sole start in points in 2017 before being sold for £275,000 later that year. He had clearly been impressing his new connections at home, sent off the 2/1-on favourite for his debut under Rules in a three-runner bumper at Worcester, and fully justified the hype to win by seven lengths. He went on to show fairly useful form in two starts over hurdles for Jonjo O'Neill, but it was when switched to Ben Pauling midway through last season that he began to really fulfil his potential.

Global Citizen beat another member of the *Fifty*—Euxton Lane—to open his account over hurdles on his debut for Pauling at Southwell in February and took the step up in grade in his stride to follow up in the Dovecote Novices' Hurdle at Kempton (by nine lengths from Scarlet Dragon) later that month, making most of the running and quickly forging clear after two out. Sent off favourite for his final start in the Top Novices' Hurdle at Aintree, he ultimately failed to repeat his Kempton form, weakening quickly in the straight, but that shouldn't detract from anything he achieved earlier in the season. Indeed, he remains a smart prospect to go to war with in the coming months, still relatively lightly raced after all, with the choice of staying over hurdles or going chasing, the latter perhaps the preferred option given how impressive he was when winning his point. **Ben Pauling**

Conclusion: *Showed smart form as a novice hurdler last season and has all the tools to make his presence felt at the top level as a chaser this time round*

Harrisons Promise   b94

6 b.m. Westerner – Hello My Lovely (Presenting)
2017/18 b16.2g³ b16s* b16.7v⁵ Jan 17

Susan Corbett only started training five years ago, starting out with eight horses, but she has built the yard year on year and now has over 30 horses in training. The expansion at her Northumberland base was given a major boost by the grant she was awarded by a European rural funding scheme in January 2017—the £9,035 she received amounted to 40% of the total project cost—and she duly enjoyed her finest season yet in 2017/18, saddling 13 winners.

One of those winners was Harrisons Promise, who built on a couple of promising efforts in bumpers to open her account at Wetherby in November. She seemed to appreciate the more testing ground that day, racing prominently and only pushed out to go clear in the final furlong, winning by nine lengths in a time much faster than the race that followed over C&D. She was quickly upped in grade after that effort and ran respectably in a listed mares' event at Market Rasen on her final start, just found out in better company. Harrisons Promise is the type to come into her own when upped in trip over hurdles this season—she isn't lacking pace but has plenty of stamina in her pedigree—whether that be in novices or handicaps further down the line. **Susan Corbett**

Conclusion: *Showed plenty in bumpers last season and is the type to make her mark over hurdles once having her stamina tested*

Kalahari Queen   h125p

5 br.m. Kalanisi (Ire) – Queen's Leader (Supreme Leader)
2017/18 h19.5d h16s* h15.7s² h18.5s* h20.5s² Mar 24

The Queen of Kalahari is a rare 342-carat diamond, which was found in the Karowe Mine in Botswana and purchased by Caroline Scheufele, the co-President of Chopard, a Swiss jewellery maker. The diamond was described as a `rare gem of exceptional beauty and purity' and part of it has subsequently been used to make the Garden of Kalahari, a necklace that weighs 50 carats.

The equine Kalahari Queen has not yet done enough to be considered a rare gem of exceptional beauty and purity, but she certainly made a good impression in her first season under Rules, winning two of her five starts. Recruited from the pointing field—she won her sole outing in that sphere—she only hinted at ability on her Rules debut, but left that form well behind when opening her account at the second attempt in a 2m novice hurdle at Lingfield eight weeks later. She was unable to follow up under a penalty on her next start, lacking the necessary gears around the tight turns of Catterick, but relished the step up to 2¼m when making a successful handicap debut at Exeter in February, staying on strongly to resume winning ways by eight lengths. She proved better than ever when finishing second to Roksana in the Mares 'National Hunt' Novices' Hurdle Finale at Newbury on her final start in March, faring best of those who raced close up with the pace, and the winner gave that form a boost when chasing home another member of the *Fifty*, Santini, on her next start in a Grade 1 at Aintree. Kalahari Queen could well stay over hurdles this season, still potentially well treated from a BHA mark of 131 after all, but the case for chasing with her is a persuasive one, a lengthy type who will not be short of opportunities in novices against her own sex. *Jamie Snowden*

Conclusion: *Point winner who progressed well in a light campaign over hurdles last season and has the scope to make a chaser; may yet prove capable of better when stepped up to 3m*

King of Realms (Ire)   h128p
6 b.g. King's Theatre (Ire) – Sunny South East (Ire) (Gothland (Fr))
2017/18 h19.3g^2 h19s^2 h19.4s* h24g Apr 18

King of Realms sounds more like a MMORPG—or massively multiplayer online role-playing game to those unfamiliar with video games—than a National Hunt performer, though it seems unlikely that anyone from the Ian Williams yard is a big enough World of Warcraft enthusiast for that to be the inspiration.

A useful bumper performer, King of Realms promised to be an interesting recruit to the hurdling ranks last season and duly shaped encouragingly in filling the runner-up spot in his first two starts in novices, when beaten two lengths at Ascot in November and getting closer still at Taunton in January, beaten three quarters of a length after looking the likeliest winner when hitting the front three out (hit 1.44 in-running). He didn't need to improve to get off the mark on his next start at Doncaster 17 days later, making the running and in control when left clear at the last. A switch to handicap company for his final start at Cheltenham followed an 82-day break, and his absence, together with a bad mistake at halfway, were perhaps the reasons for him fading in the latter stages, more so than the trip on his first try at 3m (beaten long before that could become an issue). A tall, good-topped gelding, 3m is likely to prove within his range another day, at least if his breeding is anything to go by (dam a 25f chase winner), and he remains an interesting youngster. Indeed, he is one to look out for if switching to fences this season, that appealing as by far the most suitable course of action for one of his physique. *Ian Williams*

Conclusion: *Steadily progressive in novice hurdles last term and remains open to more improvement, especially if going novice chasing; likely to stay 3m*

Lisp (Ire)   h124
4 ch.g. Poet's Voice – Hora (Hernando (Fr))
2017/18 h17.7d² h15.9s* h17.7v* h15.7v³ h16.4sᶠ Mar 14

A lisp is a speech impediment which can cause people to mispronounce certain sounds or words, resulting in unclear speech. The problem can be exaggerated in high-pressure situations—such as when the sufferer is nervous, stressed or excited—and affects people of all ages, though it is most prevalent in young children.

The Alan King-trained Lisp certainly fluffed his lines in the face of a high-pressure situation in 2017/18—he made it no further than the third before falling in the Fred Winter at the Cheltenham Festival—and it was his failure to settle down which, ultimately, prevented him from fulfilling his potential in a juvenile season over hurdles spanning five races. A fair maiden on the Flat for Charlie Hills, his keen-going nature was in evidence right from the start over jumps as he pulled his way through his hurdling debut at Fontwell in November, doing well under the circumstances to finish three and a half lengths second to Jukebox Jive. More tractable when making the most of simple tasks on his next two starts, Lisp's refusal to settle again proved his undoing when third in the Victor Ludorum Juvenile Hurdle at Haydock (pulled his way to the front after the third) in February, and it was to his credit that he might still have won but for a bad blunder two out. King reports the four-year-old to have done very well and, most importantly, relaxed more over the summer, and he looks just the sort to thrive in a big-field handicap scenario this season—he didn't get far enough to show as much in the Fred Winter. *Alan King*

Conclusion: *From a good jumping family (half-brother to the useful hurdlers Thomas Campbell and Couer de Lion) and has the physical scope to progress further himself; BHA mark of 130 looks workable*

 Follow us on Twitter @Timeform

Lord Duveen (Ire) h119p

5 br.g. Doyen (Ire) – Afdala (Ire) (Hernando (Fr))
2017/18 h16.8s⁵ h16s² Mar 17

Philip Hobbs has trained better horses since taking out his licence in 1985, but he is unlikely to have had one more genuine than the 2014 Grand National runner-up Balthazar King, who also boasted 16 wins and over £480,000 in prize money on a tremendous CV. Hobbs could certainly have done with another one like him last season; the trainer's Minehead yard suffered with a low-grade virus for most of the campaign and returned its lowest tally of winners since 1992/93. On the plus side, Hobbs has a whole host of interesting, lightly-raced horses going into this season—'In a weird way it's quite exciting, knowing that there are horses there that we haven't seen the best of,' said stable jockey Richard Johnson during the summer—and one of them is Balthazar King's close relation Lord Duveen. He laid a promising foundation for his own career when fifth in a red-hot novice hurdle at Exeter in October, not knocked about and finishing only seven and a quarter lengths behind another member of the *Fifty*, Onefortheroadtom, with subsequent Grade 1 winners Lalor and Kilbricken Storm completing the frame. Off for five months before his only subsequent start in a novice hurdle at Kempton, he again shaped well in second, still in need of the experience and almost certainly ill-served by the run of the race (outpaced in sprint finish). Needing just one more run to qualify for handicaps, he remains open to plenty of improvement, especially when stepping up in trip, and it will be interesting to see what mark he gets in that sphere when the time comes. *Philip Hobbs*

Conclusion: *Showed promise amidst greenness in two starts in novice hurdles and is one to look out for in handicaps with the prospect of more to come; likely to prove best at 2½m+ on breeding*

Adam Houghton, Content Editor (Lord Duveen): *"The Philip Hobbs yard was plagued by a virus all through last season and it may well be that Lord Duveen was unable to escape it, given that there was a five-month gap between his two starts over hurdles to date. Nevertheless, he showed sufficient promise in those outings to suggest that there are races to be won with him, especially when stepping up in trip, and Hobbs is expected to find the key to him on the back of a far more productive summer for the yard, as he did with this horse's siblings Balthazar King (Grand National runner-up) and For Good Measure (much improved in handicaps)."*

TF Download the App!

Lostintranslation offered plenty to work on over hurdles last season

Lostintranslation (Ire)   h147

6 b.g. Flemensfirth (USA) – Falika (Fr) (Hero's Honor (USA))
2017/18 h16d² h16.3d² h16.3d* h15.7v⁶ h16.4s h20s² Apr 14

For many people, cult classics Ghostbusters and Groundhog Day will be the first films that spring to mind when they hear the name Bill Murray. In terms of critical acclaim, however, his most notable role arguably came opposite Scarlett Johansson in the 2003 hit Lost In Translation; after all, it was that performance that won him a BAFTA for 'Best Actor in a Leading Role', while he was also nominated for an Oscar in the same category.

In a similar vein, Lostintranslation is unlikely to be the first horse that you think of when considering the many exciting prospects that Colin Tizzard has to go to war with in 2018/19—last season's Gold Cup winner Native River and 2016 King George hero Thistlecrack are far more likely candidates—but it could well prove folly to dismiss his awards prospects come the end of the season. After finding one too good—and showing lots of promise—in his first two starts in novice hurdles last term, Lostintranslation put his experience to good use to get off the mark at Newbury in December, making all and staying on strongly to win by three and a half lengths.

Clearly not himself at Haydock the following month, he coped well with the rise in grade when seventh in the Supreme Novices' Hurdle at Cheltenham in March and, as expected, improved further for the step up to 2½m at Aintree in April, making another member of the *Fifty*, Black Op, pull out all the stops in the Mersey Novices' Hurdle. He came a long way in a very short space of time last season and that platform is one he is expected to build on over fences this time round, with a novice chasing campaign at the top level very much on the cards. *Colin Tizzard*

Conclusion: *Form ties in well with some of the best novice hurdlers around last season, despite having just one win from six starts to his name; very much a chaser on looks and should take high rank in the novice division*

Melrose Boy (Fr) h132

6 b.g. Saint des Saints (Fr) – Pollypink (Fr) (Poliglote)
2017/18 h21.1s* h20.5s³ h21.7v* h23.4v³ h20.3v Mar 16

The horse that kickstarted Paul and Clare Rooney's interest in racing, 15-year-old Danny Zuko, now enjoys a happy retirement at the couple's property in the Scottish village of St Boswells. The same can be said of many of the horses to have subsequently graced the track in their famous blue and yellow silks, though whether the Rooneys can offer a home to all their equine retirees in the long run is questionable—they were represented by 81 horses over jumps in the UK alone in 2017/18.

There would certainly be no more fitting resident than Melrose Boy—named after the town neighbouring the Rooneys' home—when his racing days are done, and he is fancied to cement his place in their affections in the months ahead. In truth, he may have already done that having won a 19-runner conditional handicap hurdle at Cheltenham on last season's reappearance, stepping up markedly on the form he showed in 2016/17 to get off the mark (suited by the step up to 21f). He was below that level in his next two starts in novice hurdles, failing to meet expectations when third at Newbury in December and not needing to be at his best to justify odds of 10/1-on at Fontwell the following month, but raised his game again when stepped up to 23f/returned to handicap company for a valuable event at Sandown in February, keeping on well to finish three and a half lengths third to another member of the *Fifty*, Topofthegame. With excuses when disappointing on his final start at Cheltenham (struck into), he is very much the type to bounce back this season and remains on a workable mark, with the scope to make a chaser, too. *Harry Fry*

Conclusion: *Last season's third at Sandown appeals as strong form and he remains unexposed as a stayer; likely to have some big handicaps on his agenda in the second half of the season, be that over hurdles or fences*

Mister Fisher (Ire) ★   b98
4 b.g. Jeremy (USA) – That's Amazing (Ire) (Marignan (USA))
2017/18 b16s* b17s Apr 13

The Tale of Mr. Jeremy Fisher is a children's book which was written and illustrated by Beatrix Potter, and first published in 1906. The title character in the book is a frog who is forced to endure many setbacks during a fishing trip and, upon returning home, decides that he will never attempt such an excursion again. The equine Mister Fisher encountered his own difficulties last season, when finishing down the field in the Grade 2 bumper at Aintree in April, but the hope is that he will not develop such a defeatist attitude to racing, especially given the promise that he showed on his first start.

Indeed, Mister Fisher could hardly have created a better impression as he elevated himself to the upper echelon of Nicky Henderson's list of bumper horses with that comprehensive debut win at Kempton. Strong in the betting (sent off the 5/4 favourite), Mister Fisher had to overcome unfavourable circumstances to justify market expectations, held up in a race where the pace didn't pick up properly until the turn for home, quickening smartly to lead inside the final furlong and going away at the line. There were several top stables represented there, and the fourth and sixth both won next time out, so it was no surprise that Mister Fisher was sent off at just 6/1 at Aintree a month later, though, ultimately, it proved a step too far at such an early stage in his career, not unduly punished after losing his place half a mile out.

His trainer Nicky Henderson believes that Mister Fisher, who he reports to have grown considerably over the summer, 'has a bright future over hurdles', and it would be no surprise to see him deliver on his debut promise this season. By Jeremy (hence the name), who is sire of the likes of Our Conor, Jer's Girl and Whiskey Sour, Mister Fisher is expected to take high rank in the novice hurdling division, especially when stepped up in trip (plenty of stamina on dam's side of the family). *Nicky Henderson*

Conclusion: *Made good impression when winning bumper on debut last term and looks sure to improve further when going hurdling for top connections*

Moonlighter   b106+
5 b.g. Midnight Legend – Countess Camilla (Bob's Return (Ire))
2017/18 b16.7s* b16.3v⁶ Feb 10

`Sometimes it's worthwhile to do things in your own name,' said Jane Williams after announcing that the likes of Aubusson and Tea For Two would race under her name this season—rather than her husband Nick's—after taking out her own training license in August. It's therefore ironic that a horse named Moonlighter, who remains in the care of Nick, may make the biggest impression for her this season. She shares ownership of Moonlighter with his breeders Huw and Richard Davies, who also bred Moonlighter's half-brothers Horatio Hornblower, a fairly useful handicap chaser who also won twice as a hurdler, and George Nympton, a three-time chase winner who raced in the colours of The Bacchanalians, a partnership named after drunken revelry.

A glass or two was undoubtedly raised after Moonlighter's debut win in a bumper at Bangor last December. Though not usually known as a big betting yard, Moonlighter had clearly been showing the right signs at home as he was backed off the boards, looking a good prospect as he justified odds of 9/4 in a 10-runner field. Having gone with enthusiasm, he quickened to lead around two furlongs out and quickly forged clear thereafter, winning by six lengths in comfortable fashion.

Rather than try to follow up under a penalty, connections decided to pitch Moonlighter into listed company for his next start at Newbury, a race with an illustrious roll of honour and not just among the winners—Buveur d'Air, Altior, Coneygree and the aforementioned Tea For Two had all been beaten in the race before going on show top-class form over obstacles. In the event, Moonlighter shaped better than the bare result in sixth place behind Acey Milan, just not getting home faced with such a test on heavy ground. Though there is plenty of stamina in his pedigree, Moonlighter's freegoing style may mean that he's seen to best effect over the minimum trip when switched to novice hurdling this season, a division in which he looks sure to win races.
Nick Williams

Conclusion: *Found gruelling test at Newbury too much on final bumper start, but hard not to be impressed with manner of debut win; half-brother Horatio Hornblower showed best form away from the mud*

Mr Big Shot (Ire) h142p

7 br.g. Flemensfirth (USA) – Une Etoile (Ire) (Un Desperado (Fr))
2017/18 h20.3v h24.7s* Apr 14

Mr Big Shot, whose two appearances as a member of the *Fifty* last season included a 7/1 win at Aintree, has the scope to make up into an even better staying chaser this campaign. He also has the pedigree for it, being out of a sister to the useful Philson Run, winner of the 2006 Eider Chase at Newcastle.

While it's a little disconcerting that Mr Big Shot has only made it to the course a maximum of twice per season in his three campaigns to date, what's less troubling is his strike-rate: 80%. He clearly isn't one who connections want to rush, having made his debut/reappearance in March in two of his three seasons (other came in January), and that, along with the stiff examinations he was set in two starts last season, is perhaps testament to the regard in which he is held. He reappeared in the heat of

Mr Big Shot resumes winning ways at Aintree under a delighted Tom Scudamore

the Martin Pipe at the Cheltenham Festival in 2017/18, losing his unbeaten record but little caste in defeat, predictably held back by his relative inexperience in such a different environment, but still giving a clear hint as to his raw ability. He then showed the benefit of his reappearance when upped markedly in trip to 3m at Aintree, again showing residual greenness but overcoming it this time to gain a gutsy three quarters of a length win over Now McGinty, running to a smart level in the process. That the first two pulled so far clear is all to their credit, the race truly run and in a marginally quicker time than the Grade 1 over the same C&D later on the card.

Mr Big Shot must be fragile, given his size and lack of racing, but he could make a big impact over fences if he stands further training. Don't expect to see him out early, but should he progress as expected and reach the same level as he did over hurdles (BHA mark of 148), then big staying handicaps in the spring, such as the Ultima Handicap Chase at the Cheltenham Festival or the Scottish National at Ayr, would appeal as suitable long-term aims. ***David Pipe***

Conclusion: *Could make up into a leading staying novice chaser this season; potential RSA candidate if he proves too good for handicaps*

Naranja h118

6 ch.m. Black Sam Bellamy (Ire) – Full of Fruit (Fr) (Apple Tree (Fr))
2017/18 h20.5d³ h19.5s* h19.5v* h19.8v⁶ h17.7v³ h24.3g* Apr 20

Jamie Snowden had his best ever campaign last season, recording 35 wins at a strike-rate of 21%, equating to a level stakes profit of +£25.45. Amongst his list of horses with multiple victories, Naranja, or 'orange' in Spanish, pipped Our Valentina when recording a third win over hurdles at Ayr on her final start last season, and it's that performance—rather than her earlier wins on testing going at Lingfield or Chepstow—which marked her out as a *Horse To Follow* this season.

That success came over 3m, the first time Naranja had tried the trip since her hurdling debut the previous season, and it really suited—no surprise really considering her pedigree. Her dam is related to Gold Cup winner Long Run, while her sire Black Sam Bellamy can count The Giant Bolster and Sam Spinner amongst his strong-staying progeny. Naranja resumed winning ways at Ayr with a gutsy, career-best performance. Ridden prominently as is usually the case, she was left in front at the sixth and made the rest, battling well after being tackled from three out. She has the size, pedigree and attitude to do well over fences if connections decide to go down that route, while it wouldn't be a surprise to see her rise further up the hurdling ranks now that her stamina is being drawn out. *Jamie Snowden*

Conclusion: *Looks the type do well in mares' events (could run up a sequence), including if going novice chasing*

No Comment c122P

7 br.g. Kayf Tara – Dizzy Frizzy (Loup Sauvage (USA))
2017/18 c20s³ c31.8s⁶ Mar 13

"'No comment' is a splendid expression. I am using it again and again.' *Winston Churchill*

Rather than saying nothing, Philip Hobbs was more likely a little lost for words after No Comment's two efforts last season, though in hindsight he may have wished that connections had taken a more conservative approach to the horse's first campaign over fences, rather than going for the jugular from the outset. No Comment's progression over hurdles came in low-key novice events in the winter of 2016, before finishing that season with a series of good efforts in defeat at the Cheltenham, Aintree and Punchestown Festivals. In contrast, his first season over fences didn't begin until early-February, when he very much caught the eye over 2½m in the Scilly Isles' Novices' Chase at Sandown. Running over a trip that was on the short side, he took to fences well and was not at all knocked about once the first two (subsequent Mildmay winner Terrefort and Cyrname) had quickened away from him before the last. No Comment was duly stepped up in distance for the 4m National Hunt Chase at the Cheltenham Festival on his next start, but found the strong pace and soft ground too much of a test at that stage of his career. Put away after that effort, and still only seven, he remains a novice for the upcoming season and looks much more likely to do himself justice with another summer under his belt. **Philip Hobbs**

Conclusion: *Highly-tried in just two starts over fences and remains with lots of potential; from the family of Grade 1 winner Aran Concerto*

Nic Doggett (No Comment): *"There aren't too many chasers heading into this season with a 'large P' attached to their rating, but No Comment most certainly deserves his, as he's more than likely to improve significantly on his two chase starts to date. He was highly tried last term, but should be much more of a threat with his sights lowered, likely to take all the beating in novice chases before being aimed at big handicaps later in the season at the big festivals. He acts on any ground, too, so could be out earlier this campaign."*

Nube Negra (Spa) h131
4 br.g. Dink (Fr) – Manly Dream (Fr) (Highest Honor (Fr))
2017/18 h16.7g* h16.8s² h16.6s* h16.4s³ h17s⁵ Apr 12

Dan Skelton has quickly made a name for himself when it comes to transforming recruits from other yards, but he finds himself with the boot very much on the other foot ahead of this season, with several of the stable's more high-profile names having moved on to pastures new in the summer. Superb Story, who gave the yard its first Cheltenham Festival winner in 2016, and the useful mare Momella have joined Charlie Mann and Harry Fry, respectively, while Optimus Prime, fourth in the Swinton Hurdle on his final UK start, is already off the mark for his new American connections, having won the Grade 1 New York Turf Writers Cup Handicap Hurdle at Saratoga in August.

Skelton has still gained far more than he has lost from such moves over the years, and few horses in his care boast a more unusual background than Nube Negra. A maiden on the Flat in Spain, he arrived in Warwickshire to embark on a hurdling campaign in 2017/18 and quickly displayed a useful level of ability, winning a juvenile event at Market Rasen and a novice hurdle at Doncaster, either side of a highly commendable second to Apple's Shakira at Cheltenham. However, it was his effort when third in the Fred Winter at the Festival that makes him so interesting for the season ahead. Making his handicap debut, he travelled very smoothly through the race and might even have won if he'd delayed his challenge in the same way that the winner Veneer of Charm did, leading after two out before weakening on the stiff uphill finish to be beaten four lengths. Found out in Grade 1 company on his final start at Aintree, a return to handicaps should pay dividends this season, as he's a strong-traveller who looks ideal for such events over 2m. *Dan Skelton*

Conclusion: *Shaped very well when third from a BHA mark of 135 in the Fred Winter and remains favourably handicapped with the prospect of more to come after just five starts over hurdles*

Onefortheroadtom   h125

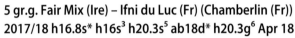

5 gr.g. Fair Mix (Ire) – Ifni du Luc (Fr) (Chamberlin (Fr))
2017/18 h16.8s* h16s³ h20.3s⁵ ab18d* h20.3g⁶ Apr 18

Former jockey Peter Turley had more than one reason to celebrate after selling Onefortheroadtom for £100,000 at the Tattersalls Ireland Cheltenham Sale in April 2017. For a start, his outlay when buying Onefortheroadtom as a three-year-old had been just €12,500, a fair profit by anyone's reckoning, but even more significant is what Turley had come through in the intervening period. Indeed, he was arguably lucky to be alive to see the sale take place at all, having taken a kick to the head from one of his father's horses just five months earlier, which resulted in him fracturing his skull, breaking an eye socket and suffering breaks to both his nose and jaw.

Few could blame Turley if he had one for the road before leaving Cheltenham—and a few more when arriving back in Ireland—and there will likely have been more celebrations when Onefortheroadtom made a winning Rules debut in a novice hurdle at Exeter in October. He looked potentially a very useful novice for Harry Fry in winning by a short-head on that occasion, finding plenty after hitting the front at the last, and there is certainly plenty of substance to the form, with the runner-up Lalor and third Kilbricken Storm both winning Grade 1s later in the campaign. Admittedly, Onefortheroadtom didn't really go on as hoped last season—his only success in four subsequent starts came in a 'jumpers' bumper' at Kempton in March—but there wasn't much wrong with his final start at Cheltenham in April, when finishing 10 and a quarter lengths sixth to Diese des Bieffes (not unduly punished), and the hope is that the switch to handicaps could be the making of him this season. A BHA mark of 137 is unlikely to prove beyond him judged on his late-2017 form alone. *Harry Fry*

Conclusion: *Strong-travelling sort who should have more to offer in handicaps at around 2½m, with a big-field scenario likely to suit; also has the physique to make a chaser (won sole start in points in Ireland)*

 facebook.com/timeform1948

Posh Trish looks set to go over hurdles this season

Posh Trish (Ire)   b107

5 b.m. Stowaway – Moscow Demon (Ire) (Moscow Society (USA))
2017/18 b17d* b16.4s* b15.7d b16v³ b17s Apr 12

For a mare with a name like hers, the handbags Posh Trish encountered on her first racecourse start in a mares' bumper at Aintree in October must have come as a horrid shock to the system. Sent off the 2/1 favourite in an 18-strong field, Posh Trish got in a fight with Grageelagh Girl more reminiscent of two school mums fighting for the last parking space at Waitrose and, ultimately, needed the help of the car parking attendant to get her way—she was awarded the race in the stewards' room after being carried left by her rival in the closing stages (passed the post a nose down). That still represented a most encouraging start to her career and Posh Trish went on to put clear water between herself and Grageelagh Girl (on 4 lb worse terms, too) when the pair met again in a listed mares' bumper at Cheltenham the following month, travelling strongly and leading on the home turn, keeping on well thereafter to win readily by three and a quarter lengths. She failed to win again in three subsequent starts, but there was nothing wrong with her third in another listed mares' event at Sandown in March, beaten only three and a quarter lengths under a penalty. An imposing type for a mare—'as much a chaser as a hurdler on looks' read the Timeform race report following her Cheltenham win—she should have more to offer as a novice hurdler for her top connections this season. *Paul Nicholls*

Conclusion: *Rangy mare who showed useful form in bumpers and looks the type to run up a sequence over hurdles this season, especially against her own sex*

Present Ranger (Ire)   h114p

5 b.g. Presenting – Papoose (Ire) (Little Bighorn)
2017/18 h16.3d⁵ h16.3v³ h19.4s³ Jan 26

Nick Skelton and Ginger McCain may have enjoyed tremendous success in their own professional careers—after all, the former was a multiple Olympic gold medallist in show jumping, while McCain's four Grand National triumphs included three with the legendary Red Rum—but both have publicly confessed that the proudest day of their lives came courtesy of their children. Indeed, Skelton was visibly moved after watching his two sons Dan (trainer) and Harry (jockey) team up to record a first Cheltenham Festival success courtesy of Superb Story in 2016, while McCain was similarly thrilled after son Donald recorded a Grand National victory of his own with Ballabriggs in 2011—'I've always said I'd like to see him win a National before I turn my toes up and he's done it,' he beamed when interviewed by the BBC in the aftermath.

Family connections run deep in National Hunt racing when it comes to both the human and equine participants, and Dan Skelton will be hoping for better things to come this season with Present Ranger, who is a full brother to none other than Ballabriggs. Runner-up on his sole outing in points, Present Ranger made an encouraging start to his career under Rules, finishing fifth in a novice hurdle and third in an introductory hurdle (both those runs coming over 2m at Newbury in December), but it was his effort when stepped up three furlongs in trip at Doncaster in January that makes him most interesting for the season ahead. Held up in the early stages, he kept on well to be beaten just eight and a quarter lengths by another member of the *Fifty*, King of Realms, showing much improved form in the process, despite still looking green. That experience is sure to have aided his development again, and now qualified for handicaps with a BHA mark of 121, he looks just the sort that could take off when stepped up further in trip. *Dan Skelton*

Conclusion: *Sturdy gelding who is very much bred to come into his own longer term, but remains open to more improvement in handicaps at 2½m+ this season*

Rather Be (Ire)   c151p

7 b.g. Oscar (Ire) – Irish Wedding (Ire) (Bob Back (USA))
2017/18 c16.1s* c17vᵘʳ c16.3s* c20.4s² Mar 13

Clean Bandit first achieved chart domination with their 2014 hit Rather Be (featuring Jess Glynne), which spent four weeks at number one and had millions humming the catchy tagline: 'When I am with you, there's no place I'd rather be'. That sentiment is one with which most loved-up individuals would whole-heartedly agree—quality time with your significant other is hugely important after all—though there are four days in March when plenty of people, at least in the Timeform offices, cannot help but prioritise form study over 'couple time'.

Form study alone would not necessarily have drawn you to the equine Rather Be ahead of his run at the 2018 Cheltenham Festival—he had faced little competition of note in three previous starts over fences, winning novice events at Towcester (by 19 lengths at 11/8-on) in December and Fakenham (by 17 lengths at 7/2-on) in February, either side of a misfortunate unseat at Plumpton. However, his light campaign was clearly a deliberate ploy by Nicky Henderson, the upshot being that he avoided a steep mark when lining up in the Close Brothers Novices' Handicap Chase at Cheltenham, and the trainer's patience was very nearly rewarded when it mattered most. Coping admirably in the face of a more high-intensity environment, jumping well and travelling strongly, Rather Be showed improved form and was only edged out by the similarly progressive Mister Whitaker close home, going down by a head. That experience should stand him in good stead this season and he looks one to follow in valuable handicap chases, still potentially well treated from just 6 lb higher than when narrowly missing out on his final start. **Nicky Henderson**

Conclusion: *Belied his inexperience when running a huge race at the Festival and should have more to offer this term; the BetVictor Gold Cup at Cheltenham's November meeting looks an obvious starting point*

Jamie Lynch (Rather Be): *"Keeping your powder dry is often a winning way in to Cheltenham handicaps, and Rather Be had industrial driers outside his stable up until March, when he failed by just a head to land the Close Brothers. The upshot of such a light and laid-out campaign is that he's still something of a 'dark' horse ahead of this season, clearly tailor-made for good handicaps from the way he tanked through the race at Cheltenham, and his re-starting point picks itself, back there for the BetVictor Gold Cup."*

Red Rising (Ire)   h139

7 ch.g. Flemensfirth (USA) – Fugal Maid (Ire) (Winged Love (Ire))
2017/18 h23.6s³ h24d* h24s² h24.1v* h22.8vᵖᵘ Mar 31

Admittedly, the countless big-race wins and 10 trainers' championships tell their own story, but there is arguably no finer example of Paul Nicholls' skill than what long-time assistant Dan Skelton has gone on to achieve. Now firmly established as one of the elite National Hunt trainers on this side of the Irish Sea, Skelton confesses to having learnt nearly everything he knows from the Ditcheat handler, a fact that was clearly not lost on Nicholls after seeing the Skelton-trained Willow's Saviour deny him a valuable win with Ptit Zig in the 2013 Ladbrokes Hurdle. 'We were watching the race together and I almost strangled him at the end,' said Nicholls in the aftermath. 'I obviously taught him too well!'

Nicholls, of course, is renowned for moulding promising young horses into high-class chasers, and Skelton will be hoping he can do likewise with Red Rising this season. A winner at the second attempt in Irish points before joining the yard, Red Rising made a winning debut under Rules in 2016/17, justifying 6/4-on favouritism in a novice hurdle at Catterick, but was not seen out again that season. He proved better than ever when winning two of his five starts last term, though, namely 3m handicaps at Southwell in December and Wetherby in February, leading before three out and staying on strongly to win by seven lengths on the latter occasion, well on top at the finish from a BHA mark of 132. He remains capable of better as a hurdler, clearly not himself when pulled up on his final start at Haydock in March, but is all over a chaser, very genuine and a thorough stayer on what we have seen so far, one who is sure to stay long distances when the occasion demands it. *Dan Skelton*

Conclusion: *Well-made gelding who looked all about stamina in hurdling starts; advancing years may hasten the decision to go chasing (relatively few miles on the clock for a seven-year-old) and one to note for a good staying handicap in the second half of the season*

Samarquand   b103p
4 b.or br.g. Malinas (Ger) – Samandara (Fr) (Kris)
2017/18 b15.3d* Apr 22

Amateur jockey Michael Legg has been lucky enough to ride some top-class horses in his career so far, not least last season's Gold Cup winner Native River, on whom he finished second in the four-miler at the Cheltenham Festival two years earlier, and the 2016 King George winner Thistlecrack. Legg enjoyed quite a close association with Thistlecrack in the early years of his career—he rode him in four of his first five starts under Rules—and can boast the distinction of being the first man to have guided him to the winners' enclosure, when landing a Wincanton bumper together in April 2014.

That same bumper was won last season by Samarquand, another horse in whom Legg has a vested interest—Samarquand is trained by Harry Fry, with whom Legg is now based, both as an amateur jockey and assistant trainer. Bought by Fry for £38,000 as a three-year-old, Samarquand went off the 5/1 third-favourite in a field of 12 for his Wincanton debut and was settled in mid-division by Noel Fehily as the runners passed the post for the first time. In a race where the gallop was only fair, there were still several in with a chance as they entered the straight, but that hope proved short-lived for backers of all bar Samarquand and Bold Plan, with that pair showing their rivals a clean pair of heels from two furlongs out, the former producing a late burst of acceleration to win by a neck. The first two should both go on to better things this season, but Samarquand deserves extra credit given that he was conceding experience to the runner-up (who had won his sole start in points) and he looks a really good jumping prospect, perhaps even more so than the same connections' Bullionaire and Caribert, both of whom were more highly-rated in bumpers. *Harry Fry*

Conclusion: *Showed impressive turn of foot when winning slowly-run Wincanton bumper and is very much one to look out for in 2m novice hurdles this season*

Sam's Gunner   h132

5 ch.g. Black Sam Bellamy (Ire) – Falcon's Gunner (Gunner B)
2017/18 h19.3s² h19.3d* h16.2v² h19.8v* h24.7sᵖᵘ Apr 13

The EBF 'National Hunt' Novices' Handicap Hurdle Final at Sandown in March is often worth more than one watch, with the race having thrown up plenty of household names over the years. Albertas Run is perhaps the best winner of the race in recent times—he emerged victorious in 2007 before going on to record back-to-back wins in the Ryanair Chase (2010 and 2011)—while The Listener, Dynaste, Many Clouds and Whisper all feature amongst those to have come up short in the race before showing top-class form when switched to fences.

That might be asking a bit much of Sam's Gunner—he won the latest renewal from a BHA mark of just 125 after all—but he does at least have the physique to suggest he could be a novice chaser to follow this season. A rangy type, he showed only modest form on his sole hurdling start in 2016/17, but proved a different proposition when stepped up to 19f on his reappearance at Catterick in January, staying on well to be beaten just a length in second, and didn't have to improve to get off the mark over C&D the following month. Another try back over 2m failed to pay dividends when second on his next start at Kelso (lacked the speed of the winner, unsurprisingly) and that experiment was quickly finished with as he made his handicap debut in the 19f EBF Final. In very testing conditions, he found plenty to lead at the last and was much the strongest at the finish, relishing the emphasis on stamina to win by seven lengths. He looks sure to stay 3m on that evidence (ran too badly to be true over that trip on his final start at Aintree) and is fancied to make hay in novice chases in the north, before testing his mettle in a big staying handicap in the spring. *Mick Easterby*

Conclusion: *Won the traditionally strong EBF Final over hurdles last season and likely to have more to offer as his stamina is further drawn out over fences*

Santini is expected to take high rank amongst the novice chasers this season

Santini ★ h150

6 b.g. Milan – Tinagoodnight (Fr) (Sleeping Car (Fr))
2017/18 h20.5d* h20.3v* h24v³ h24.7s* Apr 13

Part-owned by Richard and Lizzie Kelvin-Hughes, Thomas Campbell was one of the stars of these pages last season, progressing as expected for the step up to 3m when winning a pair of valuable Cheltenham handicaps in the autumn and, in the process, advancing his Timeform rating from 138p to 149. Still only a six-year-old, he could have even more to offer if switching to fences this season, though the Kelvin-Hughes' hardly lack for options in that department, with Santini, in particular, appealing as one who should take high rank as a staying novice chaser.

A winner of his sole outing in points before joining Nicky Henderson, Santini made the perfect start to his career under Rules in landing a novice hurdle at Newbury in December, and he looked potentially smart when following up in the Classic Novices' Hurdle at Cheltenham the following month, showing abundant stamina to overhaul another member of the *Fifty*, Black Op, close home. Henderson was minded at that time to miss the Cheltenham Festival with Santini, feeling that it might come a year too soon in his development, and the trainer's fears were realised to an extent, Santini eventually taking his chance in the Albert Bartlett Novices' Hurdle but undone by inexperience on the day, going in snatches and never nearer than the four and a half lengths he was beaten at the finish. Stamina certainly wasn't a problem on his first try over 3m and it was that quality that won him the Sefton Novices' Hurdle on his final start at Aintree, always prominent and leading after three out, finding plenty when tackled to beat Roksana by a length and a half. A strong gelding, chasing should be the making of Santini this season—'If he improves as much from this year to next year, as he did this year, then this will be an absolute machine next year,' in the words of Henderson—and there are few more exciting prospects in the novice division than him. **Nicky Henderson**

Conclusion: *Created a good impression in winning three of his four starts over hurdles last season, including the Grade 1 Sefton Novices' at Aintree, and has the build to make an even better chaser; looks worth a long-range bet for the RSA Chase at 12/1*

Soul Emotion (Fr) ★   h146p
5 b.g. Martaline – Second Emotion (Fr) (Medaaly)
2017/18 c17.9v^{pu} c18.9s^F h19.8s* h19.8s* Apr 28

A four-time winner for André Fabre in France, Martaline recorded his most prestigious victory when beating Westerner in the Group 2 Prix Maurice de Nieuil at Maisons-Laffitte in 2003. Westerner, of course, went on to prove himself much the better racehorse of the pair—he won the Ascot Gold Cup before finishing second in the Prix de l'Arc de Triomphe in 2005—but there has been very little to separate them as stallions, both sires of multiple Grade 1 winners over jumps, and it was Martaline who again had the bragging rights when two of their offspring met at Sandown in March.

In a season when Martaline was represented by two multiple Grade 1 winners in Nicky Henderson's yard, Terrefort and We Have A Dream, the exploits of Soul Emotion at the backend may have gone under the radar somewhat, but he certainly looks another exciting prospect for his sire. A fairly useful hurdler for Guillaume Macaire in France before arriving at Seven Barrows, he showed much improved form on his UK debut to make a mockery of his opening mark at Sandown, travelling strongly at the head of affairs and drawing clear before the last to win by six lengths from Westend Story (by Westerner). He was raised 12 lb on the back of that win, but that proved nowhere near enough to prevent him following up back over C&D in April, held up this time, but again travelling well and quickening clear impressively from two out to win by four lengths (with another 11 lengths back to the third) in what had looked a competitive heat beforehand. Clearly at least smart, he looks sure to develop into a graded-class performer this season, whether over hurdles or fences, the former perhaps the preferred option given that he failed to complete in his two chase starts in France. **Nicky Henderson**

Conclusion: *Looked destined for better things when annihilating handicap opposition in two starts last season and well worth a try in a higher grade at around 2½m this time round*

Step Back (Ire) c146p

8 ch.g. Indian River (Fr) – Stepitoutmary (Ire) (Roselier (Fr))
2017/18 c23.6v^2 c24.2v^3 c24.2d* c28.8d* Apr 28

For connections of Coneygree, it seems to have been one step forward and two steps back ever since he reached the pinnacle of jumps racing with victory in the 2015 Cheltenham Gold Cup. Limited to just five starts in the intervening period due to injury, the latest of which came when pulling up in the Ladbrokes Trophy at Newbury in December, the plan is for him to return this season, but it must be doubtful whether he will ever scale the same heights as he did as a novice in those few remarkable months of 2014/15.

When he does eventually retire, Coneygree will leave a mighty hole for the Mark Bradstock team, but Step Back could be up to filling it on the evidence of his own very promising novice season over fences in 2017/18, one which had connections dreaming of a tilt at the Grand National this term. Ironically for a horse of his name, he made only steps forward in a campaign that began in February, when giving best to another member of the *Fifty*, Thomas Patrick, in a novices' chase at Chepstow, and culminated with victory in one of the biggest staying handicaps of the season, the bet365 Gold Cup, just two months later (two starts in between included a novice success at Fakenham). He made such a feat look routine with a performance well beyond his years at Sandown, relishing the step up to 3½m as he defied a BHA mark of 135 in dominant fashion, always prominent in first-time cheekpieces, jumping superbly and staying on strongly to win by 13 lengths from Rock The Kasbah. He's got the tools to make it in open graded company on that evidence, but the Ladbrokes Trophy will surely be his first port of call this season and, beyond that, he'll be some sight if getting to Aintree in one piece. **Mark Bradstock**

Conclusion: *Lightly-raced sort who was most impressive when winning the bet365 Gold Cup on just his fourth chase start; 14 lb higher in the weights now, but looks sure to go on improving over fences and should be a player in all the big staying handicaps this season*

Terrefort (Fr) ★ c156p

5 gr.g. Martaline – Vie de Reine (Fr) (Mansonnien (Fr))
2017/18 c19.4s* c17.4d³ h17.9v* c21.9s³ c19.9s* c20s* c19.9s² c25s* Apr 13

In a season when Nicky Henderson was crowned the champion jumps trainer in Britain for a fifth time, it's fair to say that few horses surprised him quite so much as Terrefort. 'When he arrived at Seven Barrows if you'd have said to me he'd be contesting a Grade 1, let alone winning one, I'd be sending you to a psychiatrist,' Henderson joked in his Unibet blog prior to the horse's run in the Scilly Isles Novices' Chase at Sandown in February. 'I have to admit I'll be absolutely staggered if he's good enough to win this, certainly on what I've seen at home anyway.'

Despite his trainer's obvious misgivings, Terrefort had left his connections with little choice but to try their hand in graded company, so impressive was he when making a successful UK debut in a novices' limited handicap chase at Huntingdon in January, winning by 10 lengths from a BHA mark of 137. Henderson's comments before the Scilly Isles possibly played a part in Terrefort's market weakness on the day—he drifted from an opening show of 6/4 to an SP of 15/8—but the race quickly developed into a match between him and chief market rival (and fellow *Fifty* member) Cyrname, with Terrefort getting the verdict by a neck after a sustained duel up the straight. Second on his next start in the JLT Novices' Chase at Cheltenham, when conceding 7 lb to the winning mare Shattered Love, Terrefort was stepped up to 3m for his final appearance in the Mildmay Novices' Chase at Aintree in April and proved better than ever to resume winning ways, seeing out the longer trip really well in beating Ms Parfois by three and three quarter lengths. That performance opens up more options with regards to trip this term and the Betfair Chase looks a suitable target in the first half of the season, although his owners also have Bristol de Mai, who won the Haydock event by fifty-seven lengths in the latest campaign. In any case, Terrefort looks set to be a mainstay in the big staying chases this season when the mud is flying (raced only on soft in Britain so far). **Nicky Henderson**

Conclusion: *Won three of his four starts in novice company last season and impressed with his strong travelling, bold-jumping style; should have more to offer as a staying chaser*

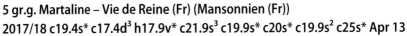

Theclockisticking (Ire) h134

6 br.g. Gamut (Ire) – Curragheen (Ire) (Sadler's Wells (USA))
2017/18 b16.7g² h16d* h15.8g* h15.7d³ h19.6s³ h20.3g²; 2018/19 h20g⁴ May 18

By and large, the UK's National Hunt trainers were a frustrated bunch last season as they waited (and waited…) for the 'Beast from the East' to make its merry way and the opportunity to unleash their horses who had been waiting for some good ground. Ultimately, that didn't happen as quickly as had been hoped—the Cheltenham Festival, for example, witnessed the softest ground at the meeting for over twenty years—and trainers were left with little choice but to run their horses in unsuitably testing conditions or wait (again) for another day.

In the case of Stuart Edmunds, he displayed a level of patience rather unbefitting for a horse with the name Theclockisticking. Second on his Rules debut in a bumper at Market Rasen in September, Theclockisticking showed useful form right from the off over hurdles, winning novices at Fakenham in October and Huntingdon (by 10 lengths under a penalty) in November, before taking the step up in grade in his stride with a good third in the Kennel Gate Novices' Hurdle at Ascot before Christmas (beaten four and a quarter lengths by another member of the *Fifty*, Claimantakinforgan). The conditions were put forward as an excuse for his below-par effort back at Huntingdon in February—'He just couldn't handle the soft ground at all,' according to Edmunds—and his wait for a sounder surface took him to Cheltenham's April meeting for his next start, where he ran another sound race when two lengths second to Diese des Bieffes. Looking ahead to this season, a BHA mark of 137 looks fair—he didn't get a chance to show as much on his handicap debut at Aintree in May (shaped well in fourth after meeting interference in the back straight)—and there should be more races to be won with him over hurdles granted his favoured conditions. *Stuart Edmunds*

Conclusion: *Tall gelding who has the scope to make a chaser, but remains unexposed over hurdles in the interim; one to note for a handicap at around 2½m in the spring*

Thomas Patrick (Ire) ★   c147p
6 b.g. Winged Love (Ire) – Huncheon Siss (Ire) (Phardante (Fr))
2017/18 h15.7d h16.8s h16.8v^2 h23.1v* h22.8v^2 h22.8v c23.6v* c30.7s^4
c26s* c25s* Apr 14

Champion jockey Richard Johnson holds the dubious distinction of the most losing rides (20) without winning in Grand National history. However, upon closer inspection, Johnson's Aintree record isn't quite so bad as that lengthy drought might imply—he's twice been runner-up (on What's Up Boys in 2002 and Balthazar King in 2014) in the National, whilst he also booted home Gower-Slave to victory in the 2001 Topham Chase.

With Native River seemingly destined for another campaign at the very top level, perhaps Johnson's best chance of Grand National success this season could come in the shape of Thomas Patrick. A winning pointer for Chris Bealby before joining the Tom Lacey yard, Thomas Patrick came a long way in a short space of time last season, making his Rules debut in a 2m novice hurdle at Southwell in October, where he beat only one home, before going on to squeeze five more runs in before the turn of the year, ending 2017 with one victory to his name, when relishing the step up to 23f to make a successful handicap bow at Exeter in November. He immediately bettered that form when switched to fences at Chepstow in February (winning by four and a half lengths from another member of the *Fifty*, Step Back, who won the bet365 Gold Cup later that season) and ended the campaign with three wins from four starts in that sphere, the latest of which came when landing a Grade 3 handicap (25f) on National day at Aintree, making all and pulling out more whenever asked, from a BHA mark of 139. Another impressive aspect of that performance—and all his starts over fences, in truth—was how well he jumped in the hands of Richard Johnson, and that should stand him in good stead in even deeper staying handicaps this season, including the big race itself at Aintree. **Tom Lacey**

Conclusion: *Tall gelding who made giant strides when switched to fences last season and should still have more to offer after just four starts in that sphere; looks tailor-made for the Grand National (thorough stayer who jumps well), with the Welsh equivalent appealing as a suitable target in the first half of the season given his ability to cope well with testing ground*

Phil Turner (Thomas Patrick): *"He enjoys bowling along and jumps well. There are lots of valuable staying chases that will really suit him in 2018/19.' That is the verdict of Richard Johnson about Tom Lacey's up-and-coming chaser Thomas Patrick and, in truth, it's hard to disagree with any of that. Indeed, it wouldn't be the biggest surprise if Thomas Patrick emerges as the horse who finally ends Johnson's long drought in the Grand National, but he'll warrant plenty of respect in big races before then, particularly when the mud is flying—the Ladbrokes Trophy (at Newbury) and Welsh National appeal as ideal targets."*

 ## Time To Move On (Ire)   b113p
5 ch.g. Flemensfirth (USA) – Kapricia Speed (Fr) (Vertical Speed (Fr))
2017/18 b16.8v* b16.8v* Feb 11

'Time to move on' are words that many an England fan will have heard this summer. As good as it was to see Gareth Southgate's side play an attacking brand of football and restore some pride to the nation, the fact that the team was less than half an hour away from qualifying for its first World Cup final since 1966 only made it more painful when it was snatched away. Alas, it was not to be, so throw the waistcoat back into the wardrobe and replace it with your thickest woolly jumper, while we explain why Time To Move On could be a novice hurdler to follow this winter.

Time To Move On is from a family that is no stranger to the *Fifty*—his half-brother Barney Dwan did a couple of good turns for these pages last season, while full-brother Cadeyrn is also nominated as a staying chaser to keep onside this time round—and it was perhaps his good jumping pedigree that saw him well-backed to turn over hot favourite Caribert on his debut at Exeter in December. He could hardly have created a deeper impression in doing so, either, forging clear late on to win by 10 lengths from the penalised Caribert, who wasn't that far below the form of his earlier victory at Wincanton and went on to win the very valuable Goffs UK Spring Sales Bumper at Newbury on his final start. Time To Move On was only seen once more himself last season, back over the same C&D as on debut, and didn't need to improve to defy a penalty, only workmanlike on the face of it but not having to be subjected to anything like maximum pressure. Admittedly, his long-term future most certainly lies over fences (described as 'a 3m chaser in the making' by trainer Fergal O'Brien), but there are still plenty of race to be won over hurdles in the interim, arguably as good a prospect for staying novices as any of last season's top bumper horses. **Fergal O'Brien**

Conclusion: *Unbeaten in two starts in bumpers and very stoutly bred; potential to make up into a leading novice hurdler this season once tackling 2½m+*

Topofthegame (pink) stays on strongly to win at Sandown

Topofthegame (Ire) ★ h154

6 ch.g. Flemensfirth (USA) – Derry Vale (Ire) (Mister Lord (USA))
2017/18 c22.4d^F h21s^4 h23.4v* h21.1s^2 Mar 14

Sadly, it was announced in April that Silviniaco Conti had died after suffering an accident during a team chasing event. A top-class chaser in his prime, he is arguably the best stayer of recent years not to have won a Gold Cup—he took a heavy fall at the third-last when travelling like the winner in 2013—but his impressive CV was none the worse for it, with seven Grade 1 wins to his name and many happy memories for trainer Paul Nicholls and part-owner Chris Giles to look back on.

The search is now on for that pair to find the next Silviniaco Conti, though they may have already done so in the shape of Topofthegame, for all that he too took a heavy fall on his sole chase start so far at Newbury in November. Switched back to hurdles for his next start in the Lanzarote at Kempton in January, Topofthegame ran a race full of promise in fourth, beaten just two and three quarter lengths and shaping as if going up in trip would see him in a better light. He duly confirmed that impression when stepped up to 23f for a valuable handicap at Sandown in February, staying on strongly to see off the attentions of Golan Fortune by a length and a half, with another member of the *Fifty*, Melrose Boy, two lengths further back in third. His best effort of last season, however, came on his final start, when beaten just a neck from a BHA mark of 150 in the Coral Cup at the Cheltenham Festival in March, doing everything right (raced smoothly/in touch) and succumbing only to Bleu Berry, who arrived much later on the scene. That effort was not far off Stayers' Hurdle standard, but it's what Topofthegame could do as a chaser this season that's the most exciting element with one of his physique (tall, raw-boned gelding), his novice status kept intact following his reappearance fall. *Paul Nicholls*

Conclusion: *Point winner who is expected improve on his smart hurdling form from last season when tackling fences this term; potential RSA candidate*

With Discretion (Ire) h134p

7 b.m. Tiger Hill (Ire) – Discreet (Kahyasi)
2017/18 h21v* h21.6s* Apr 23

According to their website, the BHA made it their objective in 2015 to 'boost the numbers of mares in training by providing a valuable and comprehensive programme of opportunities'. One of the first phases in that process has been implemented already—the inaugrual renewal of the Dawn Run Mares' Novices' Hurdle was staged at the Cheltenham Festival in 2016—and another is set to come into effect this season, with two mares' chases, the Yorkshire Silver Vase at Doncaster in December and the

Lady Protectress Chase at Huntingdon in February, both now offering £75,000 in prize money, a substantial increase compared to previous years.

Such investment—and the fact she is already seven—could hasten the decision to go chasing this season for connections of With Discretion. A maiden from three attempts in points, she justified strong support when making a winning Rules debut in a mares' novices' hurdle at Towcester in March, staying on to lead close home and appearing to have far more in hand than the length-and-a-half winning margin would suggest. However, it was her performance when following up in another mares' novice at Newton Abbot the following month that really marked her out as something to look forward to this season. Though 11 runners went to post, the race concerned only the three previous winners from a circuit out, and having made all to that point, With Discretion soon left the other pair for dead, winning by 11 lengths without getting out of second gear. She should continue to take all the beating against her own sex on that evidence, enough in it to think that she'll take to chasing (put in a slick round of jumping). *Nicky Henderson*

Conclusion: *Unbeaten in two low-key starts last term and fancied to make up for lost time this season; an exciting prospect whether remaining over hurdles or going novice chasing*

SECTION

Balliniska Band (Ire) b106

4 b.g. Vinnie Roe (Ire) – Maryiver (Ire) (Runyon (Ire))
2017/18 b16v* b16v*; 2018/19 h16s² Sep 15

The first ever to break the 29-second barrier over 500 metres, English Derby winner Balliniska Band was crowned 'Greyhound of the Year' in 1977, emulating his sire Lively Band, who had been awarded the same honour in Ireland three years earlier. Lively Band came up short in his own English Derby bid, when losing out at the semi-final stage, but he went on to prove himself an outstanding dog in his native land, when winning the Irish equivalents of that race, the 1000 Guineas and the St Leger.

The equine Balliniska Band is also by an Irish St Leger winner—Vinnie Roe won four consecutive renewals of the race between 2001 and 2004—though it is not the Classics but a jumping career that lies in store for him this season. Owned by the interestingly-named Come Home Sober Syndicate, Balliniska Band was gambled on (11/8 from 11/4) ahead of his debut in a bumper at Naas in February and duly created a really good impression in making a winning start, leading on the bridle over a furlong out and just shaken up to win by two and a quarter lengths (value for more). Stepped up in grade for his final start in a listed bumper at Limerick in April, he showed improved form to maintain his unbeaten record in comfortable fashion. Taking a wider course than most throughout, he went on over two furlongs out and impressed with how quickly he put the race to bed thereafter, winning by six lengths.

It was no surprise then, that Balliniska Band was sent off a red-hot favourite for his hurdling debut/reappearance at Listowel in September, where he shaped perfectly well after five months off, only beaten by a promising sort trained by Joseph O'Brien. Balliniska Band will have learned plenty there, and should take his form up a notch once he's stepped up in distance. **Charles Byrnes**

Conclusion: *Unbeaten in bumpers last season from two starts, seeing it out well both times in heavy ground; likely to prove best at around 2½m over hurdles*

Blackbow (Ire) b123

5 b.g. Stowaway – Rinnce Moll (Ire) (Accordion)
2017/18 b16d* b16s* b16.4s⁵ b16.3s² Apr 25

Results from the spring's big sales at Cheltenham are covered in our What's The Point feature, but the top lots from the Goffs UK Aintree Sale, held on the opening day of the track's Grand National meeting in April, could also be worth keeping an eye on if the fine record of its graduates in recent years is anything to go by. Indeed, the event has played host to some of the most exciting young names in the sport since its inception in 2016, including two members of the *Fifty*, Black Op and Topofthegame, and last season's leading novice hurdler, Samcro, whose omission from this section has more to do with our quest for something more unheralded than anything else.

Admittedly, Blackbow is a fairly obvious inclusion, too, given the promise he showed in four starts in bumpers last term, but there is no doubting that he has the potential to go to the very top in the novice hurdling division this season. Bought by the Harold Kirk/Willie Mullins combination for £150,000 at the Aintree Sale in 2017, Blackbow made a successful debut under Rules at Leopardstown on Boxing Day—the same bumper in which Mullins unleashed Champagne Fever and Bacardys—and showed much improved form to follow up in the inaugural Goffs Future Stars Bumper over C&D at the Dublin Racing Festival in February, displaying a good turn of foot to seize the initiative early in the straight and always holding on thereafter. He came up short in two subsequent starts in Grade 1 company—when fifth after refusing to settle at Cheltenham and second, having looked the likeliest winner for a long way, at Punchestown—but the regard in which he is held is obvious, with Patrick Mullins choosing to ride him ahead of several stablemates on both occasions. A good-topped gelding, jumping was always going to be his true vocation (Blackbow won his only start in points) and he can justify that belief over hurdles in the months ahead. ***Willie Mullins***

Conclusion: *Winning pointer who showed smart form in bumpers last term and should have even more to offer when going novice hurdling this season*

Blackbow (right) and Carefully Selected (middle) chase home Tornado Flyer at Punchestown

Carefully Selected (Ire)   b123

6 b.g. Well Chosen – Knockamullen Girl (Ire) (Alderbrook)
2017/18 b20s* b16s* b16.4s² b16.3s³ Apr 25

Willie Mullins was crowned champion trainer in Ireland for the eleventh season in succession in 2017/18 and the conveyor belt of talent at his Closutton base shows no signs of slowing down, with his crop of bumper horses from last term looking particularly strong. Indeed, not only did he win each of the Grade 1 bumpers in the UK and Ireland—namely the Champion Bumper at Cheltenham and the Champion I.N.H. Flat Race at Punchestown—Mullins also saddled the one-two-three in both events, all of them appearing good hurdling prospects for the months ahead.

That comment certainly applies to Carefully Selected, a well-made gelding and winning pointer who created a really good impression when making a winning Rules debut in a 2½m bumper at Leopardstown over Christmas, leading on the home turn and quickly powering clear thereafter. He appeared to relish the emphasis on stamina that day, but showed a different string to his bow when following up over 2m at Naas in February, making the running at only a steady pace and quickening up well in the straight to win readily by four and three quarter lengths. Mullins saddled five in the Champion Bumper at Cheltenham, but Carefully Selected was the pick of them on looks according to Timeform's on-course reporter and he very nearly proved so in the race, too, enterprisingly ridden from the front (gained a few lengths at the start) and still there entering the final furlong, only to be collared by Relegate close home. Again giving best only late on at Punchestown, beaten three lengths in third, he has a bright future over jumps this season and will likely prove very well suited by 2½m+. *Willie Mullins*

Conclusion: *Point winner who looked a galloper in bumpers (showing smart form) and has Albert Bartlett written all over him as he goes hurdling this season*

De Name Escapes Me (Ire)   h132

8 ch.g. Vinnie Roe (Ire) – Heartlight (Ire) (Accordion)
2017/18 c18v c22d³ c20s⁴ c16.5s h16sᵖᵘ h24d³ Apr 26

If asked 'who won last season's Champion Hurdle, Gold Cup and Grand National?', you would most likely be able to provide the correct answers—Buveur d'Air, Native River and Tiger Roll for those still wondering—without a moment's hesitation. However, change the question to 'who finished third in the 3m handicap hurdle on the third day of the Punchestown Festival?' and that's when people begin to struggle. Don't be ashamed, I came into difficulties, too. 'I'm sorry lads, the name escapes me,' I apologised meekly when asked in the Timeform offices. Strangely, my colleagues have been coming to me for my recollections of the last Irish jumps season ever since, though it has been brought to my attention that 'Not The Foggiest', 'I Don't Know' and 'That Horse of Elliott's' were not seen in action last term.

Trained by Noel Meade, De Name Escapes Me spent the first half of last season over fences, but without success, failing to win in four starts and showing only fair form when producing his best effort in a 2¾m beginners' chase at Thurles in October (beaten nearly nine lengths in third). Still out of sorts when pulled up on his return to hurdling (2m) at Leopardstown in February, he was given a break subsequently and returned after 12 weeks off to make his first start over 3m in a handicap hurdle at the Punchestown Festival, where he proved better than ever in third. He shaped very well in the event, too, making headway when badly hampered on the home turn and never nearer than the length and a quarter he was beaten at the finish, with the manner in which he saw out his race suggesting he probably would have won with a clearer run. Still totally unexposed as a stayer, he remains potentially well treated with an official rating of 130 and will be of definite interest for a similar event this season. **Noel Meade**

Conclusion: *Useful hurdler who got back on an upward curve when stepped up to 3m for the first time at Punchestown; one to note for a big staying handicap this season*

 ## Dortmund Park (Fr) h146

5 b.g. Great Pretender (Ire) – Qena (Fr) (Le Balafre (Fr))
2017/18 b11.9g* h16s⁶ h20v* h22.3v* h22s⁴ h24v h20s* Apr 27

The 2017/18 jumps season in Ireland was memorable for several reasons, with the thrilling battle for the trainers' championship between Willie Mullins and Gordon Elliott perhaps chief amongst them. However, prize money statistics can only get the blood pumping so much and, to have a truly exciting season, you need exciting races, something which we had in spades last term—for those still to be convinced, watch the closing stages of the Future Champions Novices' Hurdle at Leopardstown over Christmas or the Champion Novices' Hurdle on the final day of the Punchestown Festival in April.

The complexion of the latter race was changed dramatically by a melee at the second-last which took out three of the more fancied runners, namely Debuchet, Getabird and Scarpeta. That left 16/1 shot Dortmund Park clear in front and he stayed on strongly thereafter to win by 10 lengths from Whiskey Sour, the chief beneficiary in a similarly incident-packed renewal of the Future Champions. The odds may have suggested that Dortmund Park was a surprise winner, but he had looked a good prospect in also winning two of his first three starts over hurdles, namely a maiden hurdle at Fairyhouse and a novice hurdle at Thurles, both in January, and there were valid excuses for him disappointing in Grade 1s at both the Dublin Racing Festival (travelled best into the

Dortmund Park is one to keep onside as a novice chaser this season

straight) and the Cheltenham Festival subsequently. Indeed, the likelihood is that he was struggling with a wind problem in testing conditions and a small operation to rectify that prior to his outing at Punchestown—'We'll give him a bigger one now,' said Eddie O'Leary of owners Gigginstown Stud in the aftermath—may have been the chief reason (along with the drop back to 2½m) for the much improved display that saw him record his first win at the highest level. A good-bodied gelding, Dortmund Park is set go novice chasing this season and rates an exciting prospect for the staying division. **Gordon Elliott**

Conclusion: *Confirmed earlier promise when showing useful form to win his final start over hurdles at Punchestown and chasing could be the making of him this season; should stay 3m*

Lackaneen Leader (Ire)   h130

6 b.m. Oscar (Ire) – Shandora (Ire) (Supreme Leader)
2017/18 b16s³ h20s h18v² h16v* h20v* h22v* h20v² h24s^pu Apr 25

For every Douvan in this sport that we all love so much, there has to be a Sizing John, the perennial runner-up who could never quite get one over on his old rival. Beaten on all seven occasions that he and Douvan met, Sizing John was forced to explore new horizons in order to gain the top-level wins that his talents deserved, stepping up in trip in the second half of 2016/17 and doing so to great effect—he recorded a hat-trick of Grade 1 wins in staying chases later that season, including the biggest prize of them all, the Cheltenham Gold Cup.

Lackaneen Leader is another who could benefit from changing tack this season, with the unstoppable force that is Laurina likely to continue to prove difficult to beat in the mares' hurdling division. Admittedly, Lackaneen Leader only came up against that rival once last term, when beaten eight lengths by her in a Grade 1 at Fairyhouse in April, but that provided a more than adequate glimpse of what she can expect should she continue to bang her head against that particular brick wall, and she will be making the switch to chasing sooner rather than later. Off the mark over hurdles at the third attempt in a mares' maiden at Fairyhouse in February, Lackaneen Leader went on to win her next two starts, including a Grade 3 at Limerick the following month, and took another step up the ladder when chasing home Laurina on her first start at Grade 1 level, making her move at the same time/rate as that rival before the class divide told after two out. Possibly finding the race coming too soon when well held on her final start at the Punchestown Festival, she's got the ingredients of a high-achieving novice chaser this season (winning pointer) and looks just the type to run up a sequence against her own sex. **Gordon Elliott**

Conclusion: *Useful hurdler who should make her presence felt in the mares' novice chasing division this season*

Mind's Eye (Ire)   h139

6 b.g. Stowaway – Joleen (Ire) (Bob's Return (Ire))
2017/18 h16d² h16s* h20s* h16s h21.1s h16.5s⁴ Apr 13

`It's the first time in 15 years my brother has bought me a two-mile hurdler and he'll probably never jump a fence!' joked Michael O'Leary after Mengli Khan had won the Royal Bond Novices' Hurdle at Fairyhouse in December, his remark reinforcing the point that hurdling is normally only a means to an end so far as Gigginstown House Stud is concerned. Indeed, most of the horses that Gigginstown buys are graduates from the Irish point-to-point field, embryonic chasers whose careers over hurdles very rarely last more than one season, and there were few finer cases in point last term than the Henry de Bromhead-trained Mind's Eye.

Second on his sole start in points, the well-made Mind's Eye joined de Bromhead to embark on a career under Rules in 2016/17, filling the runner-up spot in bumpers at Naas and Thurles. Off the track for 10 months before his hurdling debut in a 2m maiden hurdle at Punchestown last October, Mind's Eye made a promising start in again finishing second, beaten 15 lengths by none other than Samcro, and didn't need to improve to go one better in a similar event at Fairyhouse in November. Upped in trip for his handicap bow at Leopardstown's Christmas meeting, he showed much improved form to defy what looked a stiff opening mark (125), leading on the bridle at the last before winning by three quarters of a length. That was to be as good as it got for Mind's Eye last season—he came up short in three subsequent starts, including in Grade 1s at the Cheltenham and Aintree Festivals—with his reluctance to settle proving as much his undoing as the exalted company. He should prove capable of holding his own at the top level another day, especially when going novice chasing (very much a chaser on looks), though his way of running means that a big-field handicap at around 2m could provide him with his optimum conditions. *Henry de Bromhead*

Conclusion: *Strong traveller who was found out at the top level over hurdles, but should do better as a novice chaser this season; the Grand Annual at the Cheltenham Festival could be a suitable target should he not come up to Arkle standard*

Next Destination (Ire)   h152p

6 b.g. Dubai Destination (USA) – Liss Alainn (Ire) (Flemensfirth (USA))
2017/18 h19v* h20v* h20v* h21.1s³ h24s* Apr 25

The second day of the Punchestown Festival proved a decisive one in determining the destination of the Irish trainers' title. Six wins on the day for Willie Mullins wiped out Gordon Elliott's lead of more than €400,000 in a matter of hours, with a Grade 1 treble from Next Destination, Bellshill and Tornado Flyer doing the most damage to Elliott's hopes of becoming champion for the first time. Next Destination, who won the Irish Daily Mirror Novices' Hurdle, was also a significant winner for his jockey, as he formed part of a treble for Paul Townend just 24 hours after he had incurred a 21-day ban for mistakenly steering Al Boum Photo around the final fence in the Champion Novices' Chase.

As for Next Destination himself, he arguably didn't get the recognition he deserved for being his stable's highest-rated novice hurdler last season. He didn't go to Cheltenham with quite the same reputation as stable-companion Getabird, who started a short price for the Supreme, or come away from it with an impressive win like Laurina. Nevertheless, he showed himself to be a smart hurdler in his own right in winning four of his five starts, including two Grade 1s, and he might well have been unbeaten over hurdles had he run in the 3m Albert Bartlett at Cheltenham and not in the 21f Ballymore Novices' Hurdle—he was initially short of pace when the tempo picked up and did his best work at the finish to be beaten less than eight lengths behind Samcro. Looking right at home over the longer trip when resuming winning ways at Punchestown, with Festival winners Delta Work (Pertemps) and Kilbricken Storm

(Albert Bartlett) completing the frame, Next Destination has the potential to take high rank amongst this season's staying hurdlers should connections decide to keep him to that sphere, though as a winning pointer his long-term future surely lies over fences. Either way, he's one to look forward to in the months ahead. **Willie Mullins**

Conclusion: *Tough sort whose only defeat over hurdles came in unfavourable circumstances; remains unexposed as a stayer and should win more races this season, whether kept to hurdles or sent novice chasing*

Paloma Blue (Ire)   h148

6 br.g. Stowaway – Court Leader (Ire) (Supreme Leader)
2017/18 h19v³ h16s² h16d* h16s³ h16.4s⁴ h16.5d Apr 24

According to the fashion label's website, Paloma Blue's collections represent 'not just a season but clothes for a way of life'. A quick browse through their catalogue reveals a distinct lack of brightly-coloured cords or tweed jackets, so the company may not count too many National Hunt trainers among their clientele, but Henry de Bromhead has always been much more understated, preferring a tried-and-tested long, dark overcoat to the pastel shades of the Home Counties.

Meanwhile, if Paloma Blue are ever interested in branching out and producing a range of rugs for horses, they could do a lot worse than get their equine namesake to model them—this lengthy sort is one of the best physical specimens in training—and he is fancied keep their name in lights with some big performances when switching to fences under the tutelage of de Bromhead this season. After chasing home Fayonagh in Punchestown's Champion Bumper in 2016/17, Paloma Blue took three attempts to get off the mark over hurdles last term, though there was certainly no disgrace in being beaten on his debut by subsequent dual Grade 1 winner—and another of our top prospects in Ireland this term—Next Destination. Paloma Blue took another step forward when third behind Samcro and Duc des Genievres in the Deloitte Novices' Hurdle at Leopardstown in February, traditionally one of the strongest races of its kind, and was then a bit too keen for his own good when a close-up fourth in the Supreme Novices' Hurdle at Cheltenham. His final start at Punchestown was too bad to be true (heavily eased off when weakening on the home turn) and, given his build, he remains a good prospect for chasing. **Henry de Bromhead**

Conclusion: *Imposing sort who kept some good company over hurdles last term and could go all the way to the top over fences; should stay 2½m when learning to settle better*

Presentimg Percy   c164p

7 b.g. Sir Percy – Hunca Munca (Ire) (Presenting)
2017/18 c22.5s* c22.6s³ c29s* h24v* c20v² c24.4s* Mar 14

Presenting Percy's entry in last season's *Fifty* described him as an exciting prospect who 'is expected to make his mark at Grade 1 level'. However, the feeling at the time was that his future was as likely to lie over hurdles as fences, given the way Presenting Percy had routed his rivals in the previous season's Pertemps Final. Though he did win the Galmoy Hurdle at Gowran in January, that run was merely a tasty surprise in a novice chasing sandwich which culminated in a roof-raising, seven-length win in the RSA Chase at the Cheltenham Festival. 'The man [trainer, Patrick Kelly] is an absolute genius,' said Presenting Percy's owner Philip Reynolds in the aftermath. 'How he hasn't got a yard full of horses is beyond me.'

Presenting Percy created a good impression on his reappearance/chasing debut at Galway in October, jumping accurately and travelling strongly en-route to a three-length win over De Plotting Shed, with the likes of Sutton Manor and stablemate Mall

Presenting Percy looks tailor-made for the Gold Cup

Dini in behind. After shaping better than the bare result when third at Punchestown the following month, Presenting Percy wasted no time getting back on track switched to a handicap at Fairyhouse in December, before that canny switch to hurdling seven weeks later. He then lost nothing in defeat when a length second to the Irish Grand National winner Our Duke in the Red Mills Chase at Gowran, after which he was sent off the well-backed 5/2 favourite for the RSA. He put up a flawless display to run out a good winner of the race historically, pushing his rating up even higher to win his first Grade 1 despite not even appearing to get near his limit (at no point out of his comfort zone). He looks sure to do better still over fences and is one to keep onside in all the big staying chases this season. *Patrick Kelly*

Conclusion: *Lots to like about his progressive, if unusual, first season over fences and looks tailor-made for the Gold Cup; unbeaten in two starts at the Cheltenham Festival*

SECTION

TALKING TO THE TRAINERS

We asked a number of leading National Hunt trainers to pick out a stable star, handicapper, and dark horse to follow for the coming season. Here's what they said ...

Harry Fry

Wins-Runs in Britain in 2017/18	**53/245**

Highest-rated horse in training	**The Last Samuri** Timeform Rating c159

Star Performer: If The Cap Fits (h149p): "He was three from three over hurdles last season before injury ruled him out of the spring festivals. We have high hopes for him as a second-season hurdler."

Handicapper: Just A Sting (h125): "A maiden over hurdles, who never seemed to get the decent ground he prefers last season. As a result, we think he could be well treated when he starts off down the novice handicap chase route."

Dark Horse: Bullionaire (b108): "A winner and runner-up in two decent bumpers, his only starts to date. He's a five-year-old who we hope can take high rank amongst this season's novice hurdlers."

Tom George

Wins-Runs in Britain in 2017/18	**47/356**

Highest-rated horse in training	**Double Shuffle** Timeform Rating c162?

Star Performer: Summerville Boy (h156p): "He has summered well and strengthened up nicely. He will more than likely be staying over hurdles this season."

Handicapper: Clondaw Castle (h129): "He never really had chance to show his true potential last season. However, we should see a lot more of him this winter over fences."

Dark Horse: Seddon (b107p): "He won his bumper in good style at Musselburgh and ran better than his finishing position suggested in the Champion Bumper. He should be an exciting novice hurdler to look forward to."

Nicky Henderson was crowned champion trainer in Britain for a fifth time in 2017/18

Nicky Henderson

Wins-Runs in Britain in 2017/18   **141/524**

Highest-rated horse in training   **Altior** Timeform Rating c179p

Star Performer: Might Bite (c171): "We were thrilled with him last season and particularly his last race when winning the Betway Bowl at Aintree following his heroic battle in soft ground in the Gold Cup. I think Aintree showed how much he has matured since his early days. The King George would be the obvious objective, but I think this year, ground permitting, we would be tempted to take in the Betfair Chase at Haydock and give ourselves a crack at the bonus. Last year he didn't run between the King George and the Gold Cup and perhaps this year we might like to get one in between the two and see what happens after that. He has summered very well and seems in great shape."

Handicapper: Rather Be (c151p): "He switched to fences last season and we had always planned to have a crack at the Close Brothers Novices' Handicap Chase at the Festival. He finished a gallant second, but that took plenty out of him and I couldn't get him back for any more. He is an improving young horse and has the potential to win a good race."

Dark Horse: Mister Fisher (b98): "I always thought Mister Fisher was one of our better bumper horses. He won well at Kempton first time out and, although disappointing in the big bumper at Aintree, I think he has a bright future over hurdles. He has grown considerably over the summer so I am hoping for a good campaign."

Philip Hobbs

Wins-Runs in Britain in 2017/18	**63/460**

Highest-rated horse in training	**Ozzie The Oscar** Timeform Rating c154

Star Performer: Gosheven (h125p): "He has not won yet, but improved massively in his three runs and hopefully might improve again to be a very decent novice hurdler."

Handicapper: Pineapple Rush (h108): "We were always pleased with her at home. We thought she was well handicapped after two wins and maybe the ground at Aintree on her last run was too quick."

Dark Horse: Gaelic Prince (h-): "He has always shown good ability at home, but got brought down at the first on his hurdling debut and then didn't run again due to a minor issue."

Alan King

Wins-Runs in Britain in 2017/18	**58/389**

Highest-rated horse in training	**Yanworth** Timeform Rating h158 c150+

Star Performer: Sceau Royal (c157): "He was a Grade 1 novice chaser last season before having a little setback in the spring, but he's back in very good form. I would like to think we can go down the 2m route. We'll probably start him off in something like the Shloer Chase at Cheltenham and see where we go."

Handicapper: Lisp (h124): "He won a couple last year and was then third in the Victor Ludorum when he didn't really settle. Unfortunately, he fell in the Fred Winter, but he's done very well this summer and he's lovely and relaxed now. Although he is on a BHA mark of 130, I think he just might be better than that. He's a big, fine horse with a lot more scope than his half-brother Coeur de Lion and I'm hoping that there's more to come with him."

Dark Horse: Giving Glances (f95): "One of my three-year-olds to go juvenile hurdling, Giving Glances has won her last two on the Flat and has a BHA mark of 85 on the level. She's schooled very well and I'd like to think she could be a pretty useful juvenile hurdler. I'll be working back from the listed race at Aintree [which King won in 2012 and 2015] in early-December."

Olly Murphy

Wins-Runs in Britain in 2017/18	**47/250**

Highest-rated horse in training	**Knockgraffon** Timeform Rating c141

Star Performer: Brewin'Upastorm (b112p): "He has very good bumper form and has summered well. He could turn out to be a very smart novice hurdler."

Handicapper: Lisheen Prince (h111): "He could turn out to be well handicapped when he goes novice handicap chasing in the depths of the winter over 3m on soft ground."

Dark Horse: Peachey (b88+): "He ran a nice race in a bumper at Market Rasen on his only start so far, showing lots of promise. He's sure to win plenty of races."

Paul Nicholls

Wins-Runs in Britain in 2017/18	**127/576**

Highest-rated horse in training	**Politologue** Timeform Rating c166

Star Performer: Politologue (c166): "He obviously had a good season last year, winning four races including the Tingle Creek. We put the tongue tie on him at Aintree, because I thought he wasn't finishing his races on a stiff track and he got the distance really well, so we're looking at going up in trip. The options at the end of November are either go 2½m at Ascot or go for the 3m Betfair Chase at Haydock, if we want to be brave. If we want a run beforehand, we could look at the Old Roan, which is something I did with Kauto Star en route to the Betfair Chase. I'm very much looking forward to him going up in trip and, if we did go for the Betfair, at least we'll know whether it's worth going to the King George—or not—fairly quick. He loves Haydock, he loves a flat track and he goes well fresh, so that might be a nice option."

Handicapper: Black Corton (c151): "He obviously had an amazing campaign and it's going to be altogether tougher for him this season, but he's a warrior of a horse. I'm thinking of going to the Future Stars at Sandown in early-November en route to the Ladbrokes Trophy."

Dark Horse: My Way (h127): "He's a maiden, but he has some high-class form in France over hurdles and fences. The plan is to go novice hurdling, start him off in a

National Hunt novice somewhere and then creep our way up. He'll hopefully win some nice hurdle races this year en route to being a nice chaser in 12 months' time."

Fergal O'Brien

Wins-Runs in Britain in 2017/18	**60/338**

Highest-rated horse in training	**Perfect Candidate** Timeform Rating c153

Star Performer: Poetic Rhythm (h137): "A real flagbearer for the yard and the Yes No Wait Sorries (owners), he became our first Grade 1 winner when taking the Challow at Newbury in late 2017. Before running under Rules for us, he won a point-to-point race at Andoversford easily and we'll be looking to go novice chasing this term. It's possible he'll start at the first Chepstow meeting at which he's been victorious in the past two seasons."

Handicapper: Lungarno Palace (h123): "Initially trained by the 'other' O'Brien in Ireland, Lungarno Palace won his first race for the stable at Huntingdon during Cheltenham Festival week. He then ran well under a penalty in his next two starts and we're hoping that this good-looking horse will be competitive in handicap hurdles this season. We may step him up in trip a little."

Dark Horse: Mount Batur (b87): "A very handsome son of Mahler who had one run for us in a bumper at Uttoxeter in November 2017, finishing a promising fourth that day. Since then we've hopefully ironed out a few physical issues and he looks great since he returned to the yard. He'll probably start off in another bumper and we're looking forward to getting him back on the racecourse."

David Pipe

Wins-Runs in Britain in 2017/18	**33/361**

Highest-rated horse in training	**Un Temps Pour Tout** Timeform Rating h162 c160

Star Performer: Un Temps Pour Tout (h162 c160): "What can I say about Un Temps Pour Tout? To land a French Champion Hurdle as well as back-to-back wins at the Cheltenham Festival is beyond anything I could have hoped for. The second of those Festival wins in the Ultima Handicap Chase, where he produced a top-class performance under top weight, took plenty out of him. He met with a setback after that which kept him off last season, but he is okay now and will be aimed at the best staying chases once again. He has always appealed to me as a Grand National type, with his blend of class, stamina and sound jumping just what you need around Aintree these days."

Handicapper: Friday Night Light (h118): "Friday Night Light was a most progressive young handicapper last season, winning at Newbury as well as finishing placed on a number of other occasions. He arguably produced his best performance when upped in trip to 19f at Ascot in February, staying on very well to finish a close runner-up in a decent handicap hurdle. He found 23f at Exeter too far last time out so will be campaigned over slightly shorter trips this time around, while he could also revert to the flat at some point. He loves soft ground."

Dark Horse: Stream Lady: "Stream Lady produced a very good first effort when bolting up in an Irish mares' maiden point-to-point. That positive view was confirmed in no uncertain terms when the second, third and fourth home all came out and won next time. She has done well over the summer and looks a most exciting type for bumpers and novices' hurdles for the season ahead.

RISING STARS

Tom Lacey

Base	**Woolhope, Herefordshire**
First Full Licence	**2014**
First Jumps Winner	**Trouble Digger** Lingfield 27/2/2013
Total Winners	**84**
Best Horse Trained	**Thomas Patrick** Timeform Rating 147p

'There are too many trainers struggling with 15 bad horses. No-one in their right minds would do it.' Tom Lacey plainly had no ambitions to take out a full training licence even after saddling a winner with his very first runner under Rules. But somewhere along the line since speaking after Trouble Digger's win in that maiden hunters' chase at Lingfield early in 2013, the former head lad to Brian Meehan and successful point-to-point handler must have had a rethink because, now a licenced trainer, far from struggling with bad horses, Lacey is fast making a name for himself with some very good ones. Lacey had 21 winners in the 2016/17 season and almost doubled that total in 2017/18 with a new best of 39, when once again backing every one of the yard's runners blind would have yielded a profit of more than £80 to a £1 stake. The yard was in particularly good form last spring, when 16 of its 30 runners were successful during a purple patch from early-March to mid-April. That run of success culminated in a couple of winners at the Grand National meeting, with the mare Jester Jet winning a Grade 3 handicap hurdle on the Friday and Thomas Patrick following suit in the Grade 3 handicap chase on the National card. That was Jester Jet's fifth win since joining Lacey little more than a year earlier, while Thomas Patrick's Aintree win took his record over fences to three out of four. Richard Johnson has ridden Thomas Patrick, one of our *Fifty*, in all his races over fences, and the partnership looks set to enjoy further success, with the Ladbrokes Trophy at Newbury (Thomas Patrick is already a C&D winner) a possible target in the first part of the season. Kateson, runner-up in the Grade 2 bumper at the Grand National meeting, looks another good prospect, with the scope to do well in novice hurdles.

Alastair Ralph

Base	**Billingsley, Shropshire**
First Full Licence	**2015**
First Jumps Winner	**Following Dreams** Leicester 12/2/2015
Total Winners	**25**
Best Horse Trained	**Cut The Corner** Timeform Rating 138

Shropshire trainer Alastair Ralph is still in the very early stages of his training career, but despite sending out only 15 individual runners in 2017/18, a strike rate of 24% for the season is one that some much bigger yards would envy. Ralph spent five seasons as assistant trainer to Henry Daly before taking out his own licence, and also had spells working for Paul Nicholls and Dr Richard Newland. Before gaining a full licence, he had success with pointers, notably Following Dreams, who at 50/1 chased home On The Fringe in the 2015 Foxhunter at the Cheltenham Festival. The same horse had landed a gamble in a novices' hunters' chase at Leicester the previous month, when becoming Ralph's first winner under Rules. The majority of the yard's winners to date came in 2017/18, which began well when the stable registered its first double—courtesy of Gustave Mahler and It's Oscar—at Worcester within weeks of the campaign getting underway. Other highlights included Bob Ford making a successful debut for the yard in a veterans' chase at Chepstow in October, landing another gamble in the process, while later in the season Comber Mill ran up a hat-trick in handicap hurdles. By the end of the summer the stable had notched another five wins, so Ralph should be well on course to better last season's total of 14 this term. Two of the current season's wins were provided by the stable's best horse, the useful chaser Cut The Corner who won handicaps at Newton Abbot and Stratford, while another came from Newt in a mares' handicap hurdle at Uttoxeter, a track where the stable has now won with five of its 11 runners to date.

Dylan Robinson

Attached Stable	**Henry de Bromhead**
First Ride	**2015**
First Winner	**Damefirth** Kilbeggan 17/07/2015
Total Winners	**35**
Best Jumps Horse Ridden	**Balko des Flos** Timeform Rating 166

Speaking in an interview with Horse Racing Ireland ahead of the 2017 Cheltenham Festival, Dylan Robinson was on tenterhooks waiting to see if the opportunity to ride at the meeting for the first time would present itself. 'I'm holding out for a spin in the Martin Pipe Conditional Jockeys' Handicap Hurdle on the last day,' he said. 'It's everyone's dream to ride there and my agent Ciaran O'Toole is on the case. He has done very well for me so far this year and hopefully he'll come up trumps for Friday!' Sadly for Robinson, his agent was unable to secure him a ride on that occasion, but the young man from Waterford's patience—which was tested further by a broken wrist he suffered in June 2017, ruling him out for five months—was rewarded last season with two rides at Cheltenham. Conrad Hastings was pulled up in the Close Brothers Novices' Handicap Chase, but he guided Discorama to second behind Blow By Blow (beaten five lengths) in the latest renewal of the Martin Pipe. Robinson spent time with Dermot Weld and Jim Bolger in the early stages of his career (rode nine winners on the Flat before switching codes), but he is now based with Henry de Bromhead, who has provided him with 26 of his 35 winners over jumps to date, including his first wins over both hurdles (on Damefirth at Kilbeggan in July 2015) and fences (on The King of Brega at Limerick in July 2016). He has not been short of outside rides either—'I must have ridden for nearly every trainer in the country,' reckons Robinson—and it is a sign of the regard in which he is held that Gordon Elliott, Jessica Harrington and Noel Meade all utilised his talents last season. His tally of 12 winners in that campaign was only two shy of his previous best in 2016/17, when he achieved some notable landmarks including riding his first double (at Fairyhouse on New Year's Day) and losing his 7 lb claim, and there is no doubting that he would have done better last term but for his injury woes. Indeed, he is already well on his way to his best season yet in 2018/19, with eight winners on the board at the time of writing, including a first success in Britain aboard Ornua at Newton Abbot in July, and he is likely to have got a particular thrill from riding the one-time high-class Sub Lieutenant in the Galway Plate, the pair beaten a little over 11 lengths in fifth.

Harry Stock

Attached Stable	**Martin Keighley**
First Ride	**2014**
First Winner	**Franciscan** Sedgefield 04/04/2014
Total Winners	**26**
Best Jumps Horse Ridden	**Brillare Momento** Timeform Rating 133

'Some would not have come back from the injury he had,' said Martin Keighley after his young conditional Harry Stock had won aboard Bobble Emerald on just his second Cheltenham mount last October. Stock's story is a remarkable one. In January 2015, when based with Donald McCain, a horse fell on Stock during a schooling session, breaking the young rider's back. After eight screws and two rods were inserted to repair the injury, Stock was confined to his bed for months, leaving him wondering whether he would ever ride again. Having missed the whole of the 2015/16 season, and 18 months in total, a resilient Stock returned to action for McCain the following season, before moving down south to join Keighley in Gloucestershire, where he quickly built up an excellent relationship with the mare Spice Girl. Indeed, Stock is in exalted company, with champion jockey Richard Johnson the only other rider to record a win on the horse. Stock guided Spice Girl to two bumper wins in July 2017, but it was Johnson's absence after being stood down through injury at Towcester which led to the association being continued over hurdles the following November. Stock received a late call-up, rushing to the track to make it in the nick of time for the ride on the hurdling newcomer. Despite some novicey errors and a slow jump at the last, Spice Girl won, leading Keighley to describe the young conditional as 'a big asset to our yard and super value for his 7 lb claim too'. With that in mind, Stock's relatively new association with jockey-turned-agent Ian Popham should ensure plenty of good outside rides this season, and he has already teamed up with Tony Carroll for a win this summer aboard Vive Le Roi, a horse who hadn't won since March 2016. 'Days like this are why you come back,' said Stock after his Cheltenham win last October; he should enjoy plenty more in the spotlight over the coming years.

ANTE-POST BETTING

Timeform's Chief Correspondent Jamie Lynch takes a look at the markets for some of the feature races in the National Hunt calendar and picks out his value bets...

Stable tours aren't interesting
Every horse reconditioning.
'They've grown overnight.'
What a load of shoptalk.
Jumping is the winter wonderland.

Gone away is the blue-blood
Here to stay is the deep mud.
Goodbye to Flat speed
Hello cords and tweed.
Jumping is the winter wonderland.

And at Haydock we can build a snowman
From the snow and frost lying around.
We'll say 'are you Kirkland?'
He'll say 'no man.
But you can guarantee it's heavy ground.'

Later on, we've got Cheltenham,
English town, Irish welcome.
To watch fall away
Our ante-post play.
Jumping is the winter wonderland.

Welcome to the winter wonderland of the 2018/19 National Hunt season, and our long-term look at matching the right faces to the right races as a means of unearthing some ante-post value. Ah, value. Like those un-Christmassy Christmas presents where somebody sponsors an animal on your behalf, or you 'buy' some phoney-baloney title for your Dad or some non-existent star for your Mum, 'value' is a hollow gift, providing nothing material, no matter how much thought goes into it.

All the same, the thought that goes into it is stimulating, the hope that goes with it is invigorating, and the rewards at the end of it are game-changing, potentially at least. Therefore, with belief and bravery, if fortune does indeed favour the brave, let's gallop through the staying chase that is the jumps season and count on clearing at least one of the financial fences.

Ladbrokes Trophy

That's the Ladbrokes Trophy which will forever in our hearts and minds be spelled H-E-N-N-E-S-S-Y. The rebranding is a sore point because the race has great heritage and history, a heritage and history that gives the race great importance, as well as great value, swelled to a gilt-edged, guilt-edged £250k by the good people of Ladbrokes, and that combination of lore and lolly was the reason Willie Mullins wrapped up his best-handicapped horse for it last year, Total Recall duly delivering, before contesting the Gold Cup and Grand National in the spring.

If not the Grand National, then the Gold Cup is certainly pencilled in for stable-companion Al Boum Photo for this season, but before then he looks a perfect fit for this high-end handicap, whether it's based on the one-year trend of the Ladbrokes Trophy or the six-decade history of the Hennessy. Whereas one good turn deserves another, one wrong turn in racing means another will never happen again, such as the wrong turn taken by Paul Townend approaching the final fence in the Champion Novices' Chase at Punchestown, steered right to audience amazement, costing Al Boum Photo a Grade 1.

He took Finian's Oscar down with him, and Robbie Power was adamant that he'd have won without being carried out by a carried-away Townend, but review it and judge for yourself, to see if you agree with me that Al Boum Photo was in Rick Astley-mode and never gonna give it up. If the question was describe his campaign in one word, 'lucky' would be a Pointless answer, as he could easily have won two other races he didn't, having been in command when falling at the last in a Grade 2 at Limerick on Boxing Day and giving a head start to Monalee when beaten just three-quarters of a length by him in the Flogas. And yet Al Boum Photo still managed to grab a Grade 1, at the expense of Cheltenham winner Shattered Love, at Fairyhouse in April, as not just a silver lining but also a sign of things to come, tailor-made for a Hennessy—or indeed a Ladbrokes Trophy—being a classy second-season chaser with some hidden depths.

SELECTION: **Al Boum Photo (16/1)**

The Nationals

The reason for this wider-encompassing sub-category is that Thomas Patrick has his name on a National this season, very possibly the Welsh version, for which there's no ante-post market as yet, but you know what to do when one bookmaker pops up (and the rest all line up in the same formation, as seems the modern way), and for now we'll have to make do with backing him—at 40/1—for the big one itself.

Timeform trust in form and titter at fate, but there was something fateful about Thomas Patrick winning at Aintree on Grand National day in 2018, over conventional fences, though soaring over said conventional fences with a poise and purpose that meant he was already eyeing up The Chair and Becher's Brook on his way around. Remarkably, that authoritative, all-the-way win in a good-class handicap came just six months on from his debut under Rules, and only two months after his first steeplechase, snowballing in strength and status once combining forces with Richard Johnson, the pair made for each other.

Thomas Patrick won three of his four starts over fences last season

His first season racing was a triumph, at the same time just a trial, in training for the marathons that are mapped out in his diary, and the fact he's so low on mileage and high on potential marks him out from the staying crowd. We'd be staggered if Thomas Patrick didn't win a 'National' in the 2018/19 season, partly as there's now so many of them, but more so as there are so few contenders like him, a usual suspect in one sense but unusual in another, given the trajectory he's on. Aintree is the absolute ambition, but Chepstow is an achievable aim, and, as far as the Welsh National is concerned, it's fastest finger first for refreshing Oddschecker. Good luck with that on beating us bots at Timeform to the punch.

SELECTION: **Thomas Patrick (40/1, Grand National)**

Arkle Chase

The Samcro Resolution. Not the title of the next Bourne film but the punting predicament, as referenced in the RSA section, regards the repetition of Samcro at the top of various Cheltenham markets while his short-term strategy is still to be announced. The Arkle, though, is low on the likelihood list, as sticking to two miles probably means sticking to hurdles, for the Champion itself, while the purpose of a chasing programme would be to prepare him for a Gold Cup the season after, thereby sending him down the staying road. Not that the Arkle desperately needs Samcro, not with the classy cast assembling for an autumn audition.

In fact, the initial auditions for the Arkle tend to take place on the Tuesday of Cheltenham the year before, and, sure enough, the runners-up from both the Champion Hurdle (Melon) and Supreme Novices' Hurdle (Kalashnikov) are reportedly readying themselves for the switch to fences.

There's a bit of a theory at Timeform, perpetuated by the older, wiser, balder heads, that free-going hurdlers make better chasers, the bigger obstacles serving to increase their respect and decrease their impatience, enabling a performance that's more efficient, therefore, more expressive. If there's anything in that hypothesis then it will apply to Paloma Blue, whose hurdling career was compromised by his headstrong ways, nonetheless finishing fourth—just three lengths behind Summerville Boy and the aforementioned Kalashnikov—in the Supreme. The fact he's in the Henry de Bromhead academy, where chasers come first, an unofficial strapline for the stable, adds weight to the belief that Paloma Blue could prove a different proposition over fences, which could be some sight remembering he was knocking on the Grade 1 door in bumpers and novice hurdles.

SELECTION: **Paloma Blue (25/1)**

National Hunt Chase

The poorest relation of the novice chases at the Festival is the National Hunt Chase, which is kind of like saying that the poorest relation of the Kardashians is Rob, as it's still worth plenty. The four-mile distance means it's survival of the fittest, or sometimes the slowest, and many have cried enough by the time the climax unfolds, an end game that impacts the start point in the season, as there aren't too many first-season chasers that can have a path plotted to the National Hunt Chase safe in the knowledge they've (probably) got what it takes. But Blow By Blow is one of them.

Taking his staying power on trust might seem odd about a horse who was so good in bumpers (two miles) and sharp enough to make all over two-and-a-half miles at last year's Cheltenham Festival (Martin Pipe Handicap Hurdle), though the swan-like Blow By Blow works overtime beneath the surface, and such propulsion is stamina in a different manifestation, but stamina all the same, as likely to be exercised at four miles as two.

And then we come to the positives of his trainer, not only as Gordon Elliott has trained three of the last eight winners of the National Hunt Chase, but also because the temptation to target the RSA with Blow By Blow won't be so strong when Team GG (Gordon and Gigginstown) have other high-flying arrows to fire for that, headed by Cracking Smart, Delta Work and Champagne Classic. Blow By Blow has only twice

Blow By Blow on his way to victory in the Martin Pipe

raced beyond twenty furlongs so far, winning the first time and over the top for the season when misfiring in a Grade 1 at Punchestown last April, but that—and fences—is where his future lies, worth a punt that he gets as far as the National Hunt Chase.

SELECTION: **Blow By Blow (25/1)**

RSA Chase

There are lots of hurdling heavyweights with an eye on the RSA prize if they can cut it as chasers, maybe including the biggest and best of all of last season's novices, Samcro, who remastered and revamped the Public Enemy track to 'make it his own' as Simon Cowell would say. Do Believe The Hype.

However, pre-empting the programming of the SatNav is half the battle of ante-post betting, and whereas Samcro has dozens of destinations to choose from, hurdles and fences, Santini seems more single-minded, because since day one he's looked every inch an RSA horse of the future. And this is the season when his future becomes the present, and his price is our present.

'Day one' was as recently as December 1st, 2017, but he came with a reputation, embellished by a point-to-point win, and his only misstep in his novice season was when beaten favourite (into third, undone by inexperience) at the Cheltenham Festival, soon putting that right in a Grade 1 at Aintree a month later. Number three in the inaccurate racing clichés chart (behind 'the good'uns go on any ground' and the front-running fiction of 'doing it the hard way') is usually the well-worn line of 'whatever 'X' does over hurdles is a bonus,' the theory being that a horse will suddenly transform from Clark Kent into Superman for having something bigger to jump. I say 'usually' because there are some times, albeit rarer than reported, when it's true, and surely it will be true of Santini given his size and shape, so much a chaser on looks that our racecourse representative noted it at Newbury on December 1st, on day one. If you back one horse out of this long-range preview, make sure it's Santini for the RSA, as all his ingredients—from his background to his barn and his build—mark him out as something special for chasing, to the extent that it's easy to envisage him going off 5/2 favourite at Cheltenham on Wednesday, March 13th.

SELECTION: **Santini (12/1)**

Ryanair Chase

A championship event that occupies the middle ground is always going to vary in quality, hence the Ryanair takes more winning in some years than others: a Timeform rating of 159 secured victory for Dynaste in 2014, while Vautour hit the heights of 180 two years later. If the formidable Footpad flies Ryanair next spring, then we're talking Vautour numbers, in which case an open race will become a closed shop, but to focus on the what-ifs with Footpad—and same goes for Samcro—is to forget the primary purpose of ante-post wagering, of taking a risk, not of risking the takings.

Hope for the best; plan for the worst. Long-range betting doesn't plan for the worst, and the best-case scenario for Benatar is for him to continue his flight path from last season, before landing on a run-of-the-mill renewal of the Ryanair. And there's more chance of that happening than his current odds of 40/1 would imply.

He was only a five-year-old when charged with chasing, and charged through his first three races, leaving Finian's Oscar chasing at Ascot. A three-month break ahead of the JLT at Cheltenham freshened him up, too much so, as his in-built enthusiasm spilled over into eagerness, pulling hard, and, under the circumstances, finishing third—to Shattered Love and Terrefort—was an achievement, more so considering he was found to be lame. His big engine needs a little fine-tuning, but that he's got a big engine is the pertinent point, and time is on his side, because youth is on his side, included in our *Fifty* for that very reason.

SELECTION: **Benatar (40/1)**

Cheltenham Yankee

Champion Hurdle: Samcro 7/1

Gold Cup: Presenting Percy 6/1

Mares Hurdle: Laurina 3/1

RSA Chase: Santini 12/1

Finally, for a more conservative, but equally rewarding, multiple bet to keep us warm through the winter, here's a fantastic foursome who could and should all end up favourites for their respective races should everything go smoothly. We've skirted around Samcro in previous paragraphs, but there's logic to backing him for the Champion Hurdle. First things first, Samcro is a sensation, living up to the hype and then some, all the way up until his uncharacteristic leaping lapse at Punchestown, and the fact he contested the Champion there was a statement, as well as a sign. His management team are clearly convinced he could win a Champion Hurdle, as are we, and the temptation to prove the point may be irresistible. And if he did, instead, set foot down the chasing road, reverting to hurdling remains an option (in the 0.01% chance he doesn't take to fences).

Native River and Might Bite had a doozy of a duel in the 2018 Gold Cup, the former's stamina smothering the latter's speed, but, 48 hours earlier, Presenting Percy showed Might Bite's speed and Native River's stamina in running away with the RSA, looking in control every inch of the race, and looking every inch a Gold Cup winner of the future. His approach to Cheltenham may once again be unorthodox, but his ambition is clear, along with his agility and ability, potentially too hot for the older guard to handle.

Bar Altior and Buveur d'Air, there aren't any shorter-priced favourites in the ante-post lists than Laurina, but you're basically banking on her heading to the Mares' Hurdle, as what's going to beat her in that? Nothing. Quevega is the prime example of Willie Mullins' MO of largely letting his good mares win the good mares' races, rather than mess with the males, and, only a five-year-old, there's time for all that in later seasons for Laurina. And the compelling case for Santini was spelled out in the RSA write-up, well worth including him in any money-making multiple. Winning big is the punting promised land, and jumping is the winter wonderland.

WHAT'S THE POINT

The Brightwells Festival (March) and April Sales at Cheltenham are two of the best opportunities to buy horses who have made bright starts to their careers in points, with several members of the *Fifty*—including Claimantakinforgan, Posh Trish and Santini—amongst those to have changed hands there in recent times. Business at the two events was again buoyant earlier in the year, so let's look at the key lots who could make their mark under Rules for new connections in the coming months...

The top lots at the Cheltenham Festival Sale both went the way of Gordon Elliott, with **Andy Dufresne** and **Feel My Pulse** each costing him £330,000. The team at Cullentra House can already boast the inside track on Andy Dufresne, as he was trained by Elliott to win his point at Borris House six days prior to the sale. Consigned by Elliott's travelling head girl Camilla Sharples, the trainer must have been unable to convince her to sell privately, but both will have been happy with the eventual outcome, as Andy Dufresne is set to stay in the yard in the ownership of J.P. McManus, while Sharples suggested in the immediate aftermath that she would put the money towards a new house!

A day after Andy Dufresne won on his debut, Feel My Pulse also made a winning start in a five-runner maiden at Lismore, forging 15 lengths clear of the runner-up. He looks another top prospect from the same source, Monbeg Stables (run by brothers Donnchadh and Sean), that has produced the dual Cheltenham Festival winner Holywell, Grand National runner-up The Last Samuri and one of this season's most exciting novice chasing prospects, Claimantakinforgan, in recent years.

Overall, Monbeg Stables sold four lots at the sale, with Harold Kirk and Willie Mullins—not to be outdone by his chief rival for the Irish trainers' championship—stretching to £230,000 for **The Big Getaway**. He made a successful debut in points at Horse and Jockey (by a distance) earlier in March and is one to look out for over hurdles when the season proper begins, a comment that also applies to the remaining two lots sold by the Doyles, five-length Ballyarthur winner **Brewers Project** (£185,000) and **Bubbles of Gold** (£60,000), who won his point by eight lengths at Lingstown. The former went the way of Paul Nicholls and Tom Malone, who paid £135,000 for Posh Trish at the corresponding sale 12 months earlier, while Bubbles of Gold, by the same sire as Holywell in Gold Well, is set to go into training with Olly Murphy.

The Mullins/Kirk combination also came away with **Ontheropes** (£240,000) and the French-bred **Elite Charboniere** (£155,000). The former is a son of Presenting (from the family of the Grade 1 placed hurdler Gentle Buck) who missed out only narrowly on his sole start in points at Punchestown in February, while Elite Charboniere showed the benefit of his initial experience when impressively winning a bumper at Seiches-Sur-Le-Loire, also in February.

Also worth a mention is **Interconnected**, who was sold to Highflyer Bloodstock for £220,000 following a wide-margin win on his second point start (fell on debut) at Larkhill in February. Highflyer bought Mr Whipped—a useful novice hurdler for Nicky Henderson last season—for £160,000 at the corresponding sale 12 months earlier and that horse's half-brother **Tippingituptonancy** was another of this year's top lots. Tim Vaughan and Select Racing were the successful buyers on this occasion, with a bid of £185,000 enough to secure Tippingituptonancy following a promising second in his debut point at Horse and Jockey. Overall, there were 14 six-figure lots at the Festival Sale, with one of the last to go through the ring, **The Captains Inn**, adding his name to that list when selling to Stroud Coleman Bloodstock for £220,000; he offered plenty to work on when a three-length second on his sole outing in points at Lingstown earlier in the month.

The victor that day was **Thatsy**, who was led out unsold when offered for £145,000 himself at the Festival Sale. He boosted his reputation when beaten just a head in a winners' race at Loughanmore three weeks later and was eventually found a home—and not just any home—when returning to Cheltenham for the April Sale, with that man Gordon Elliott stretching to £130,000 to add the four-year-old to his ever-expanding string.

The general feeling was that the latest April Sale was down on quality compared to previous years, with Thatsy one of only two lots to break through the six-figure barrier—there were 12 in 2017. The other was **Cobbler's Way**, who made £120,000 for the same Milestone Stables (run by Colin Bowe) that sold Samcro at Aintree in April 2016. Cobbler's Way is bred to be a stayer, from the family of the high-class chaser Foxchapel King, and it was over 3m that he made his point debut 11 days before the sale, when finishing a length and a half second at Dromahane.

The best price for a member of the fairer sex was achieved by the four-year-old Fame And Glory filly **Deja Vu**, who was consigned by Aidan Fitzgerald's Cobajay Stables and arrived on the back of a win in a four-year-old mares' maiden point at Inch in March. Anthony Honeyball was the successful bidder at £82,000, a significant increase on the €15,000 Fitzgerald paid for her at the Derby Sale 10 months earlier.

Others to keep an eye on for new connections in the coming months, both on pedigree and performance, include **Redzor** and **Kiltealy Briggs**. From the family of Death Duty and Foxrock, the former opened his account at the third attempt in points at Ballyragget in March and was a £80,000 buy for owner Brian Drew and Tom Malone. The latter was also involved in the £70,000 purchase of Kiltealy Briggs, this time in conjunction with trainer Jamie Snowden. Kiltealy Briggs was beaten a neck on his only start at Inch at the end of March and is the first foal out of an unraced full-sister to the Grand National winner Ballabriggs.

SECTION

TIMEFORM'S VIEW

Chosen from the Timeform Formbook, here is Timeform's detailed analysis—compiled by our team of race reporters and supplemented by observations from Timeform's handicappers—of a selection of key races from the Cheltenham and Aintree festivals last spring.

CHELTENHAM Tuesday March 13
SOFT

Sky Bet Supreme Novices' Hurdle (Grade 1) (1)

Pos	Btn	Horse	Age	Wgt	Eq	Trainer	Jockey	SP
1		SUMMERVILLE BOY (IRE)	6	11-7		Tom George	Noel Fehily	9/1
2	nk	KALASHNIKOV (IRE)	5	11-7		Amy Murphy	Jack Quinlan	5/1
3	1¾	MENGLI KHAN (IRE)	5	11-7	(t)	Gordon Elliott, Ireland	J. W. Kennedy	14/1
4	1	PALOMA BLUE (IRE)	6	11-7		Henry de Bromhead, Ireland	Davy Russell	14/1
5	2¼	CLAIMANTAKINFORGAN (FR)	6	11-7		Nicky Henderson	Nico de Boinville	16/1
6	2¼	WESTERN RYDER (IRE)	6	11-7		Warren Greatrex	Richard Johnson	20/1
7	¾	LOSTINTRANSLATION (IRE)	6	11-7		Colin Tizzard	Robbie Power	40/1
8	2¼	SHARJAH (FR)	5	11-7		W. P. Mullins, Ireland	P. Townend	20/1
9	1¾	DEBUCHET (FR)	5	11-7		Ms Margaret Mullins, Ireland	D. E. Mullins	20/1
10	22	SIMPLY THE BETTS (IRE)	5	11-7		Harry Whittington	Sean Bowen	40/1
11	9	GETABIRD (IRE)	6	11-7		W. P. Mullins, Ireland	R. Walsh	7/4f
12	19	US AND THEM (IRE)	5	11-7		Joseph Patrick O'Brien, Ireland	J. J. Slevin	28/1
13	½	KHUDHA (IRE)	4	10-13	(s)	Alan Fleming, Ireland	Denis O'Regan	200/1
14	1	SAXO JACK (FR)	8	11-7	(t)	Sophie Leech	Sean Houlihan	200/1
15	2¼	GOLDEN JEFFREY (SWI)	5	11-7		Iain Jardine	Conor O'Farrell	150/1
F		SLATE HOUSE (IRE)	6	11-7	(t)	Colin Tizzard	Harry Cobden	20/1
pu		DAME ROSE (FR)	5	11-0	(t)	Richard Hobson	Jonathan Burke	40/1
pu		FIRST FLOW (IRE)	6	11-7		Kim Bailey	David Bass	12/1
pu		SHOAL BAY (IRE)	5	11-7	(t)	Colin Tizzard	Tom Scudamore	80/1

19 ran   Race Time 4m 05.60 Closing Sectional (4f): 61.5s (97.4%) Winning Owner: Mr R. S. Brookhouse

While clearly Getabird, the by-now regulation Mullins-trained favourite for the Supreme, failed to give his running, this looked a more competitive race than the market suggested, and the form of the good novice races through the winter was broadly represented, the first 2 having contested the Tolworth Hurdle in January, the third runner-up to Getabird at Punchestown, the fourth behind Samcro in the Deloitte; it was run at a sound pace, in similar fashion to the later Champion Hurdle, the time comparing favourably, suggesting this is solid if not outstanding form, though the winner would have scored much more decisively had he not made a complete mess of the second-last. **Summerville Boy** improved again, confirming Sandown placings with the runner-up and doing particularly well to get back into the race after what might well have been a chance-ending mistake 2 out; held up, not always fluent, travelled well, good progress fifth, close up when blundered 2 out, lost place, rallied well straight, third when mistake last, found plenty to lead close home; he's taken really well to hurdling, but he looks a chaser and the Arkle rather than the Champion Hurdle ought to be his destination next season. **Kalashnikov** is growing up all the time, this his best performance yet, a more forward ride looking to benefit him, going through the race better than he had on either of his last 2 starts, though unable to reverse placings from Sandown with the winner; close up, travelled well, led 2 out, ridden straight, kept on well, headed close home; he's a likeable type and seems sure to continue to give a good account, his stamina still to be drawn out. **Mengli Khan** in first-time tongue strap, gave a boost to the favourite's form, even though that one didn't himself; prominent, chased leader after 2 out, challenged last, not quicken final 100 yds; he's a different type in terms of background to the others in the frame, and may not have quite their potential to progress next season. **Paloma Blue** just about the pick on looks, ran a fine race in defeat, building on his effort behind Samcro last time, helped by a truer pace, but still a bit keen for his own good; prominent, not settle fully, not quicken after 2 out, rallied run-in; he could yet improve further over hurdles and will make a smashing chaser when the time comes. **Claimantakinforgan** ran at least as well as previously and shaped a bit better than the distance beaten suggests too, his effort delayed longer than perhaps ideal; raced off the pace, still plenty to do before 3 out, ridden after 2 out, stayed on; he's done well over hurdles this season and may well do even better as a chaser down the line. **Western Ryder** produced a career best, despite being significantly hampered at the second-last, likely to have finished fifth without that; held up, took keen hold, effort when hampered 2 out, plugged on straight; he will probably benefit from a return to further. **Lostintranslation** ran well upped in grade, clearly not himself last time; raced off the pace, not fluent fourth, headway before 2 out, not quicken straight; he remains with potential to improve when he steps up in trip. **Sharjah** contesting a third successive Grade 1 novice, got back on track, proving at least as good as ever; held up, effort before 2 out, one paced approaching last; he's raced solely at around 2m on soft going so far, this probably his limit under such circumstances. **Debuchet** runner-up in the 2017 Champion Bumper, had a bit to prove after just 2 runs over hurdles and wasn't ready for the task at this stage, perhaps the ground plenty soft enough for him as well; handy, effort 2 out, weakened run-in; he remains with potential. **Simply The Betts** was well held, an optimistic runner at this level; held up, pushed along fifth, never on terms; he's been highly tried over hurdles and could do with being given a more realistic campaign. **Getabird** proved a disappointment, the performance of the third suggesting he ought to have been competitive, possibly better going right handed; led, joined fourth, fifth (jumped right), not fluent 2 out, headed, soon done with, eased approaching last; he's worth another chance at this level, with options back the other way round at Fairyhouse and Punchestown next month. **Us And Them** failed to take the eye beforehand and was well held under a change of tactics, needing to improve to figure anyway; in touch, chased leaders after fifth, ridden 3 out, weakening when blundered next. **Khudha** found the whole thing well beyond him; novicey mistakes, always behind. **Saxo Jack** was well out of his depth; always behind. **Golden Jeffrey** had shown nothing to justify his place in this field; always behind. **Slate House** in a tongue strap, was in the process of running creditably when departing, not so good as his defeat of the winner here in the autumn makes him look; mid-field, took keen hold, mistake second, ridden after 2 out, held when fell last; he has plenty about him physically and it would be no surprise to see him make a better chaser next season. **Dame Rose** was predictably found wanting at this level in first-time tongue strap after 7 weeks off; prominent, took keen hold, lost place fifth, left behind next, pulled up straight. **First Flow** disappointed after 8 weeks off, faced with much the sternest test of his short career, badly let down by his jumping; close up, mistake second, disputed lead fourth and fifth, where jumped badly right, weakening when blundered 2 out, pulled up; he looks the part for chasing and ought to make the grade in that sphere next season. **Shoal Bay** was simply outclassed; held up, struggling when mistake fifth, lost touch after, pulled up next.

Racing Post Arkle Challenge Trophy Novices' Chase (Grade 1) (1)

Pos	Btn	Horse	Age	Wgt	Eq	Trainer	Jockey	SP
1		FOOTPAD (FR)	6	11-4		W. P. Mullins, Ireland	R. Walsh	5/6f
2	14	BRAIN POWER (IRE)	7	11-4		Nicky Henderson	Nico de Boinville	14/1
3	¾	PETIT MOUCHOIR (FR)	7	11-4		Henry de Bromhead, Ireland	Davy Russell	4/1
4	38	SAINT CALVADOS (FR)	5	11-4		Harry Whittington	Aidan Coleman	11/4
5	71	ROBINSHILL (IRE)	7	11-4		Nigel Twiston-Davies	Sam Twiston-Davies	66/1

5 ran   Race Time 4m 02.30   Closing Sectional (3.75f): 57.1s (100.1%)   Winning Owner: Mr Simon Munir/Mr Isaac Souede

A 5-runner Arkle, the smallest field in the history of the race, but the quality was good with the 3 highest-rated novice chasers of the season to now over any trip taking each other on and Footpad ran out a most impressive winner, putting up a top-class performance not dissimilar to that the likes of Un de Sceaux, Douvan and Altior did in winning the event in recent years; it must be said that an overly-strong pace set things up perfectly for such a wide-margin success and Walsh excelled on Footpad, sitting well off the duelling pair up ahead, biding his time, whilst Davy Russell and Aidan Coleman can be criticized for tearing off on Petit Mouchoir and Saint Calvados, the former doing well not to crack sooner. **Footpad** couldn't have had a better set-up scripted, his 2 main rivals cutting each others throat, but rather than flattering him the scenario simply provided a platform for him to fully showcase his talent and, make no mistake, this was a performance out of the top drawer as he maintained his unbeaten chase record; he raced in touch early but was sensibly held back off the leading pair, travelling strongly, a blunder as he let fly at the sixth no more than a momentary scare, immediately back on the bit and easily making headway before 4 out, close up at the next and in front before 2 out, clear by the last and staying on strongly for all that his rivals were mostly tired; aside from that one forgiveable lapse, Footpad's jumping was as slick and efficient as it had been previously, that one of the key factors in his rapid progress since switched to fences, although he 's also probably more the finished article physically and mentally than in previous years, only 6 yet at his third Cheltenham Festival; short term he'll continue to be very hard to beat and this is evidence that he'll ruffle feathers in what could be a red-hot 2m division at the top end next season, but he does stay further (won a Grade 1 hurdle over 19f as a 4-y-o) and going up in distance in this sphere is a possibility too. **Brain Power** picked up the pieces on the day, benefiting from the overly-strong pace, but we have enough evidence already to know that he's full value for this rating and it's a positive that he completed on the back of an unseat/fall and finished off his race, his first since a wind operation; his rider wanted nothing to do with the early pace, dropping him out and allowing Brain Power time to get into a rhythm, keeping mistakes to a minimum and making headway after 4 out, held at the last and hanging left but running on once pulled off the rail and taking second late on; he's not a top-notcher but is still developing as a chaser and this good run in a high-intensity environment should give him confidence moving forward. **Petit Mouchoir** is always likely to be in the shadow of Footpad over fences but the distance between them at Punchestown last month is perhaps a truer reflection of the class differential as he shaped clear second best here but paid the price for going off too hard; soon led, headed fourth, led again before sixth going with zest, clear 4 out, reduced advantage before next, headed before 2 out, held when mistake last, no extra, lost second near finish; he's only 3 starts into his chase career and has the opportunity and potential still this season to match his high-class hurdles form. **Saint Calvados** showed at Warwick that he's a high-class novice, that big performance backed up by the clock, and there was more to this than him not coping in an even tougher race, not helped by the ride, but moreover something seemed amiss, cutting out quickly; led until first, remained prominent, led again fourth, headed again before sixth, lost touch between 4 out and 3 out, tailed off. **Robinshill** was out of his depth and simply couldn't cope from an early stage, not jumping well and always behind.

Unibet Champion Hurdle Challenge Trophy (Grade 1) (1)

Pos	Btn	Horse	Age	Wgt	Eq	Trainer	Jockey	SP
1		BUVEUR D'AIR (FR)	7	11-10		Nicky Henderson	Barry Geraghty	4/6f
2	nk	MELON	6	11-10		W. P. Mullins, Ireland	P. Townend	7/1
3	3	MICK JAZZ (FR)	7	11-10	(h+t)	Gordon Elliott, Ireland	Davy Russell	25/1
4	9	IDENTITY THIEF (IRE)	8	11-10		Henry de Bromhead, Ireland	Sean Flanagan	50/1
5	1¾	ELGIN	6	11-10		Alan King	Wayne Hutchinson	12/1
6	8	FAUGHEEN (IRE)	10	11-10	(s)	W. P. Mullins, Ireland	R. Walsh	4/1
7	½	WICKLOW BRAVE	9	11-10	(b)	W. P. Mullins, Ireland	Mr P. W. Mullins	14/1
8	1¼	CH'TIBELLO (FR)	7	11-10		Dan Skelton	Harry Skelton	33/1
9	17	JOHN CONSTABLE (IRE)	7	11-10	(t)	Evan Williams	Leighton Aspell	66/1
pu		CHARLI PARCS (FR)	5	11-10		Nicky Henderson	Noel Fehily	100/1
pu		YORKHILL (IRE)	8	11-10		W. P. Mullins, Ireland	D. J. Mullins	14/1

11 ran Race Time 4m 05.10 Closing Sectional (4f): 61.1s (97.8%) Winning Owner: Mr John P. McManus

Hardly a vintage Champion Hurdle but an exciting race, truly run, and it drew performances from the first 2 that place them at the head of the 2m hurdle rankings this season, only Irish Champion Hurdle winner Supasundae, the most notable absentee, having rival claims to that position, the 3-time runner-up My Tent Or Yours withdrawn on the day another who would have added depth. **Buveur d'Air** back to defend his crown after landing all 4 races in the meantime, maintained his winning sequence in rather grittier fashion than has become the norm, having to knuckle down to hold on after the last, perhaps the softer ground at this level not in his favour, the lack of a serious race in the build-up perhaps a factor as well, a good chance that he will step forward at Aintree; handy, travelled strongly, led 2 out, shaken up straight, edged ahead final 50 yds. **Melon** finally showed the sort of form his reputation suggested he could, well supported this time, the hood left off, the good pace (lacking in the International) almost certainly in his favour, some scrimmaging with Faugheen after 3 out not making any real difference; in touch, travelled strongly, closing when hampered soon after 3 out, upsides next, ridden approaching last, kept on, held final 50 yds; he'll presumably get the chance to go one better at Punchestown. **Mick Jazz** proved better than ever, running a similar race to last time, just not able to land a blow at the first 2; held up, travelled well, headway before 2 out, ridden straight, not quicken last. **Identity Thief** took another step forward, running his best race since spring 2016, clearly still capable of smart form; chased leaders, not always fluent, lost place after third, kept on straight. **Elgin** was supplemented for this after his win at Wincanton, but more was needed at this level and he wasn't able to raise his game to the degree required; waited with, travelled well, headway when shaken up 2 out, not quicken straight, never landed a blow; he reportedly could switch to the Flat, his level of ability suggesting he'd be a serious player in good handicaps once qualified. **Faugheen** in first-time cheekpieces, was possibly unsettled by the pacemaker and not helped by the headgear, the old spark just not there, though it should be pointed out that he'd finished in front of the trio behind the winner at Leopardstown last time; led first, pressed leader until fourth, not fluent next, led soon after 3 out, wandered, headed 2 out, left behind soon after. **Wicklow Brave** returned to hurdling in this after a run in the Melbourne Cup for the second season running, but he didn't fare so well as he had in 2017, after 4 months off, away on terms this time, but his finishing effort again lacking. **Ch'tibello** had run creditably in several trial races this season, but without showing nearly enough to suggest he was up to the task, though he reportedly finished sore; held up, never on terms. **John Constable** wasn't likely to be good enough, the ground in a more competitive race a side issue; held up, left behind before 2 out. **Charli Parcs** served his turn as pacemaker, disrupting Faugheen, his job done by 3 out; took keen hold, led after first, clear after fourth, headed soon after 3 out, weakened quickly, pulled up before last. **Yorkhill** had won at each of the last 2 Festivals, but he hasn't looked himself this season and, back over hurdles for the first time since 2016, he never looked likely to get involved, pulled up before the last.

CHELTENHAM Wednesday March 14
SOFT

Ballymore Novices' Hurdle (Baring Bingham) (Grade 1) (1)

Pos	Btn	Horse	Age	Wgt	Eq	Trainer	Jockey	SP
1		SAMCRO (IRE)	6	11-7		Gordon Elliott, Ireland	J. W. Kennedy	8/11f
2	2¾	BLACK OP (IRE)	7	11-7	(t)	Tom George	Noel Fehily	8/1
3	5	NEXT DESTINATION (IRE)	6	11-7		W. P. Mullins, Ireland	R. Walsh	4/1
4	nk	SCARPETA (FR)	5	11-7		W. P. Mullins, Ireland	D. E. Mullins	33/1
5	1	DUC DES GENIEVRES (FR)	5	11-7		W. P. Mullins, Ireland	P. Townend	10/1
6	¾	VISION DES FLOS (FR)	5	11-7	(t)	Colin Tizzard	Robbie Power	14/1
7	14	AYE AYE CHARLIE	6	11-7		Fergal O'Brien	Conor Shoemark	100/1
8	sh	GOWITHTHEFLOW (IRE)	5	11-7		Ben Pauling	Daryl Jacob	40/1
9	2¼	BRAHMA BULL (IRE)	7	11-7		W. P. Mullins, Ireland	D. J. Mullins	25/1
10	9	MIND'S EYE (IRE)	6	11-7		Henry de Bromhead, Ireland	Davy Russell	66/1
11	2¼	DIABLO DE ROUHET (FR)	5	11-7		Jo Hughes	Mark Grant	200/1
12	2½	COOLANLY (IRE)	6	11-7		Fergal O'Brien	Paddy Brennan	100/1
13	16	KNIGHT IN DUBAI (IRE)	5	11-7	(t)	Dan Skelton	Harry Skelton	100/1
pu		AHEAD OF THE CURVE (FR)	6	11-7	(s+t)	Susan Corbett	James Corbett	200/1

14 ran Race Time 5m 18.70 Closing Sectional (3.9f): 57.5s (102.3%) Winning Owner: Gigginstown House Stud

Samcro was just about the most talked-about horse of the whole Festival build-up, not least whether he would contest this race or the Supreme—that discussion not one fuelled by connnections, it's fair to say, this always the target, despite a win at 2m in the Deloitte—and he didn't let his fans down, producing the best performance in this race since Faugheen, just having too much speed and class for the pair that chased him home, that pair at least with pretentions to this level, a fair few of the others clearly overfaced, Samcro's task here probably easier than it would have been in the Supreme. **Samcro** had looked a really exciting prospect in winning his first 3 starts over hurdles and outclassed this field, not having to improve significantly from his form in the Deloitte but still having plenty more to offer as he is further tested; mid-division, tanked along, headway before 3 out, led after next, ridden run-in, kept on well; his future is bursting with possibility, so many options with regard to trip and obstacles, fingers crossed that he is able to deliver. **Black Op** shaped really well, no match for the winner but beating the others readily enough, still not the finished article; handy, travelled well, mistake third, keeping on when mistake last, stuck to task; he very much looks the part for chasing and will be an exciting novice over fences next season. **Next Destination** ran creditably, though connections surely missed a trick, running here rather than in the Spa, short of pace when the tempo picked up, doing his best work at the finish; held up, outpaced 3 out, kept on well straight, took third final 100 yds; he remains open to improvement as his stamina is drawn out. **Scarpeta** a different type to most of these, raced on the Flat, seemed to excel himself, up markedly in trip, on just his third start over hurdles, but he was well positioned and may be flattered just a shade; close up, ridden before 2 out, not quicken approaching last; he's a smart novice, his future probably in good handicaps, rather than fences or anything better. **Duc des Genievres** had been no match for Samcro at Leopardstown, so it was no surprise he came up short, even back up in trip, though he ran as well as previously; held up, travelled well, headway before 3 out, shaken up before 2 out, not quicken straight; he may be able to find a race at a slightly lower level in the spring and is a likely sort for chasing next season. **Vision des Flos** ran well upped in grade, well served by the return to a longer trip; handy, took keen hold, led briefly 2 out, one paced straight; he's bordering on smart as a novice hurdler, but will surely be even better as a novice chaser, presumably in the autumn. **Aye Aye Charlie** was overfaced yet again and ran about as well as could be expected, surely better campaigned at a more realistic level; held up, headway when mistake 3 out, ridden after, no extra. **Gowiththeflow** was essentially found out in better company, not able to go with the principals after dictating; led until before 2 out, weakened before last. **Brahma Bull** down in trip after 4 months off, ran to a similar level as on his hurdling debut, his lack of experience evident; waited with, ridden when no room end of back straight, soon done with; he remains with potential. **Mind's Eye** was up against it back in novice company; held up, took keen hold, shaken up before 2 out, made little impression; he's very much a chaser on looks. **Diablo de Rouhet** predictably made little impact; raced off the pace, ridden before 3 out, never on terms. **Coolanly** was set a very stiff task on just his second start over hurdles and was well held after 3 months off; prominent, mistake fifth, weakened 3 out; he may yet do better in calmer waters. **Knight In Dubai** is a useful novice, but this grade is beyond him; held up, pushed along before seventh, left behind 3 out; he looks the sort to make a better chaser. **Ahead of The Curve** turned in a lifeless effort, even allowing for the grade; held up, mistake fourth, lost touch soon after, pulled up next.

RSA Insurance Novices' Chase (Grade 1) (1)

Pos	Btn	Horse	Age	Wgt	Eq	Trainer	Jockey	SP
1		PRESENTING PERCY	7	11-4	(t)	Patrick G. Kelly, Ireland	Davy Russell	5/2f
2	7	MONALEE (IRE)	7	11-4		Henry de Bromhead, Ireland	Noel Fehily	10/3
3	7	ELEGANT ESCAPE (IRE)	6	11-4		Colin Tizzard	Harry Cobden	9/1
4	1½	BALLYOPTIC (IRE)	8	11-4		Nigel Twiston-Davies	Sam Twiston-Davies	9/1

TIMEFORM'S VIEW

5	1¾	BLACK CORTON (FR)	7	11-4	(t)	Paul Nicholls	Bryony Frost	5/1
F		AL BOUM PHOTO (FR)	6	11-4		W. P. Mullins, Ireland	R. Walsh	8/1
F		BONBON AU MIEL (FR)	7	11-4	(t)	W. P. Mullins, Ireland	P. Townend	33/1
pu		ALLYSSON MONTERG (FR)	8	11-4	(t)	Richard Hobson	Jonathan Burke	50/1
pu		DOUNIKOS (FR)	7	11-4		Gordon Elliott, Ireland	J. W. Kennedy	12/1
pu		FULL IRISH (IRE)	7	11-4	(s+t)	Emma Lavelle	Leighton Aspell	100/1

10 ran   Race Time 6m 32.10   Closing Sectional (3.75f): 57.8s (104.4%)   Winning Owner: Philip J. Reynolds

The standard and competitiveness of staying novice chases in Ireland this season has been higher than in Britain, and this first Anglo-Irish clash in the division confirmed as much, the upshot a strong RSA in terms of the rating achieved by the winner, the Irish trio that came into the race with the best form set to fill the 1-2-3 when Al Boum Photo fell at the second last; Black Corton set the pace and ensured an honest gallop without charging off and it wasn't until after 4 out that the race started to develop properly. **Presenting Percy** had plenty in his favour, top-rated after a progressive campaign in Ireland, and he put up a flawless display to run out a good RSA winner, pushing his rating up even higher to win his first Grade 1 despite not even seeming to get near his limit, at no point out of his comfort zone; held up, jumped well and travelled strongly, good progress after 4 out, produced to lead before 2 out, clear last, stayed on well; he'll need to improve again out of novice company next season but looks a tailor-made Gold Cup horse, a course specialist (also won the Pertemps Final at this meeting in 2017) with laden stamina. **Monalee** came up against an above-average winner of this race, his own performance on par with some other recent winners at the lower end of the scale, doing all he could in that he barely put a foot wrong and was produced to have every chance; never far away, jumped well in main, went with enthusiasm, led 3 out, headed approaching 2 out, kept on but no match for winner. **Elegant Escape** has held his form well all season and this was an improvement for all that he was beaten 14 lengths, faring best of the British and shaping like a thorough stayer, this barely enough of a test; chased leaders, ridden after 4 out, outpaced between 3 out and 2 out, kept on well; he has time on his side, younger than the other finishers here, and will definitely be suited by long distances, likely to come into his own in some of the top-end staying handicaps next season, maybe even a Welsh National type for instance. **Ballyoptic** was in by far his toughest chase yet and ran well without being a match for the best of the Irish staying novices; chased leaders, not always fluent, ridden before 3 out, outpaced before home turn, kept on; there's still room for improvement in his jumping, but he isn't a liability on that score and still has longer distances to explore in this sphere. **Black Corton** has had a fantastic season, but it's fair to say that the British staying novice division has been relatively uncompetitive and he was found out in this; led, made mistakes, headed 3 out, held when left in a place 2 out, weakened run-in; it's been a long season for him, too, and he may be at a further disadvantage going into the spring with so many others having been kept fairly fresh. **Al Boum Photo** was in the process of running creditably when departing, held in third when falling 2 out, set to finish in that position, but it wasn't his first error (blundered 4 out) and he'll need to improve on that front if he's to achieve what he might as a chaser; he didn't get chance to confirm his stamina but should stay 3m. **Bonbon Au Miel** was found out in better company after bolting up in a relatively uncompetitive maiden when last seen 8 weeks ago; mid-division, not settle fully, lost place around halfway, weakened 3 out, behind when fell last; it is still early days but he's yet to stand regular racing. **Allysson Monterg** was out of his depth; raced off the pace, off the bridle before most, beaten soon after 4 out. **Dounikos** was closely matched with Monalee and Al Boum Photo on a couple of pieces of form this winter but disappointed, possibly not handling the track; mid-division, lost place soon after 4 out, well beaten next, pulled up; he should stay 3m. **Full Irish** who wore first-time cheekpieces, was flying too high in this grade and it showed throughout, jumping ponderously in rear, struggling badly by the fourteenth and pulled up soon after a blunder 4 out.

Betway Queen Mother Champion Chase (Grade 1) (1)

Pos	Btn	Horse	Age	Wgt	Eq	Trainer	Jockey	SP
1		ALTIOR (IRE)	8	11-10		Nicky Henderson	Nico de Boinville	1/1f
2	7	MIN (FR)	7	11-10		W. P. Mullins, Ireland	P. Townend	5/2
3	11	GOD'S OWN (IRE)	10	11-10		Tom George	Paddy Brennan	40/1
4	5	POLITOLOGUE (FR)	7	11-10		Paul Nicholls	Sam Twiston-Davies	12/1
5	12	ORDINARY WORLD (IRE)	8	11-10		Henry de Bromhead, Ireland	Davy Russell	40/1
F		CHARBEL (IRE)	7	11-10	(s)	Kim Bailey	David Bass	28/1
F		DOUVAN (FR)	8	11-10		W. P. Mullins, Ireland	Mr P. W. Mullins	9/2
pu		AR MAD (FR)	8	11-10	(s)	Gary Moore	Joshua Moore	50/1
pu		SPECIAL TIARA	11	11-10		Henry de Bromhead, Ireland	Noel Fehily	25/1

9 ran Race Time 4m 06.00 Closing Sectional (3.75f): 56.6s (102.5%) Winning Owner: Mrs Patricia Pugh

This promised to be one of the highlights of the whole jumping season and didn't disappoint, Altior powering away in the closing stages from a rival who himself was finishing off well, gaining a third successive victory at the Festival and confirming himself the best horse in training, and, for all it would have been even better had Douvan completed, still tanking along when he departed, he would have needed to be at least as good as ever to deny Altior—the winner isn't so good as Sprinter Sacre at his best, but this performance is on a par with the next best performances in this race this century, up there with the likes of Master Minded's demolition job in 2008 and Moscow Flyer's defeat of Well Chief in 2004 for his second win, Min running to a level good enough to have landed a few recent runnings himself; incidentally, it has been mentioned that the overall time was slow, compared to the previous day's Arkle, but, leaving aside the dubious merit of merely comparing raw times on 2 different days, the Arkle was the first race on this track and 3 large fields completed 5 circuits of it later that afternoon, so the ground would have been well churned up compared to the Arkle, while it was pretty still that afternoon, whereas this day was very windy. **Altior** confirmed his status as the best 2m chaser around, arguably the best jumper of any description, with an ultimately totally dominant performance, even if it didn't look all that likely 3 out, powering up the hill, just as he had when winning the 2016 Supreme and 2017 Arkle, the first coincidentally also by 7 lengths from Min; in touch, jumped fluently, pushed along after tenth, chased leaders straight, switched 2 out, led soon after last, stayed on strongly, impressive; he may be a little more fragile than this suggests—he was subject of a scare at the start of the week, when reported lame at exercise—but hopefully there will be other days when he can show just how good he is. **Min** produced a performance good enough to have won several recent editions of this race and indeed looked to set to do so 3 out, clearly going best at that stage, before he was overpowered by Altior in the straight, just as he had been in the 2016 Supreme—he's a top-class jumper, but Altior is a better one; held up, travelled strongly, smooth headway 3 out, led 2 out, ridden when headed soon after last, kept on well, no match for winner. **God's Own** had missed his chance in this race last season, when mistakes were costly, as he was just outclassed in a stronger renewal this time round, for all that his rider had something of a rush of blood to the head 4 out, still only third with a more measured ride; held up, rapid headway approaching tenth, left second there, led after 3 out, headed when mistake next, not quicken, kept on run-in; he's a regular in the Melling Chase, winning it in 2016, and will presumably go there next. **Politologue** had done well, kept busy, when Altior was absent in the autumn, but he'd been put firmly in his place by him at Newbury and it was a similar story here, just swept away, in better form than the distances indicate; held up, headway seventh, left in front tenth, headed after 3 out, chased leaders still next, no extra before last. **Ordinary World** had plenty to find, even on his best form, and finished well held, though he was competitive until 2 out and remains in form; in rear, hampered sixth, good progress 3 out, close up when mistake next, no extra. **Charbel** after 3 months off, failed to complete, ridden more patiently than for his 2 previous Festival visits; in touch, fell sixth. **Douvan** hadn't been seen since flopping so dismally in this 12 months previously, but he was looking much more his old self until departing, under Patrick Mullins, a last-minute replacement for the injured Walsh, still full of running but probably doing plenty, given the circumstances; prominent, went with zest, led eighth, fell tenth; hopefully he can return at Punchestown, if not before, and show just how good he is these days. **Ar Mad** didn't run much of a race in first-time cheekpieces after 3 months off, though there was plenty about the race that wouldn't have suited him, including the opposition; close up, jumped right, labouring after seventh, pulled up after 4 out, reportedly lame. **Special Tiara** had won this 12 months previously, but with Douvan flopping that was a much weaker renewal than this one and he was well beaten when his rider drew stumps; led, clear briefly fourth, mistake fifth, headed eighth, hampered tenth, slow 3 out, pulled up straight.

Weatherbys Champion Bumper (Standard Open National Hunt Flat) (Grade 1) (1)

Pos	Btn	Horse	Age	Wgt	Eq	Trainer	Jockey	SP
1		RELEGATE (IRE)	5	10-12		W. P. Mullins, Ireland	Ms K. Walsh	25/1
2	nk	CAREFULLY SELECTED (IRE)	6	11-5		W. P. Mullins, Ireland	D. E. Mullins	6/1
3	3¼	TORNADO FLYER (IRE)	5	11-5		W. P. Mullins, Ireland	P. Townend	14/1
4	1¾	ACEY MILAN (IRE)	4	10-11	(t)	Anthony Honeyball	Aidan Coleman	9/2f
5	½	BLACKBOW (IRE)	5	11-5		W. P. Mullins, Ireland	Mr P. W. Mullins	5/1
6	1¾	FELIX DESJY (IRE)	5	11-5	(h)	Gordon Elliott, Ireland	Keith Donoghue	8/1
7	½	COLREEVY (IRE)	5	10-12		W. P. Mullins, Ireland	D. J. Mullins	50/1
8	1½	MERCY MERCY ME	6	11-5		Fergal O'Brien	Paddy Brennan	25/1
9	1¼	RHINESTONE (IRE)	5	11-5	(t)	Joseph Patrick O'Brien, Ireland	Barry Geraghty	5/1
10	3¼	DIDTHEYLEAVEUOUTTO (IRE)	5	11-5		Nick Gifford	Mark Walsh	12/1
11	hd	THE BIG BITE (IRE)	5	11-5		Tom George	Noel Fehily	20/1
12	1¼	SEDDON (IRE)	5	11-5		Tom George	A. P. Heskin	33/1
13	3¾	DASHEL DRASHER	5	11-5		Jeremy Scott	Matt Griffiths	100/1
14	9	KNOW THE SCORE (IRE)	5	11-5		David Pipe	Tom Scudamore	20/1
15	nk	ARCH MY BOY	4	10-11		Martin Smith	Leighton Aspell	100/1
16	1½	STONEY MOUNTAIN (IRE)	5	11-5		Henry Daly	Andrew Tinkler	100/1
17	1	JAYTRACK PARKHOMES	4	10-11		Colin Tizzard	Harry Cobden	80/1
18	3¾	VOLCANO (FR)	4	10-11		Nigel Twiston-Davies	Sam Twiston-Davies	50/1
19	3	NESTOR PARK (FR)	5	11-5		Ben Pauling	Daryl Jacob	100/1
20	1½	THE FLYING SOFA (FR)	5	11-5		Gary Moore	Jamie Moore	66/1
21	9	DOC PENFRO	6	11-5		Kevin Frost	Brian Hughes	200/1

22	48	CROOKS PEAK	5	11-5	Philip Hobbs	Richard Johnson	25/1
pu		THEBANNERKINGREBEL (IRE)	5	11-5	Jamie Snowden	Gavin Sheehan	33/1

23 ran Race Time 4m 04.60 Closing Sectional (3.9f): 56.4s (103.1%) Winning Owner: Mr Paul McKeon

A typical field on paper for the premier bumper of the whole season, all bar 2 of the runners having won at least once, 14 of them unbeaten, though loads looked to have plenty to find to be competitive and it is unlikely to go down as a vintage renewal, for all that it will throw up the usual host of novice hurdle winners next season, too many relatively close up for that to be the case and those with the best form seeming a little below their best; however, it was notable for the dominance of one stable, Willie Mullins enhancing his already superb record in the race by filling 5 of the first 7 places with his 5 runners, the only other 2 Irish-trained runners also in the first 9 home, the result a rout for the home contingent, the favourite Acey Milan faring best, though beaten fair and square; the first 2 home were ridden in starkly contrasting fashion, the winner last for much of the way and still only fourteenth over 1f out, the runner-up well away and dictating under a well-judged ride, if anything the winner deserving marking up a little. **Relegate** has improved significantly from run to run and did so again, producing a remarkably strong finish after being only fourteenth over 1f out, in much the same style as the winning mare of last year, the ill-fated Fayonagh; in rear, pushed along over 4f out, still plenty to do home turn, stayed on strongly over 1f out (drifted left), led close home; she looked very much a stayer and so is likely to want further next season. **Carefully Selected** progressed again and, while that owed something to his rider's enterprise, there was still plenty to like about the performance; broke fast, led, went with zest, quickened home turn, ridden over 1f out, hung right, kept on well, collared close home; he was the pick of the Mullins team on looks and surely has a bright future over jumps. **Tornado Flyer** improved significantly on his debut form, taking the rise in class in his stride, looking the main threat to the runner-up at one point, possibly being less experienced than the first 2 a factor; waited with, travelled well, headway approaching straight, ridden over 1f out, not quicken, kept on well inside final 1f. **Acey Milan** was unable to extend his winning run to 4, a little below the form he showed at Newbury, though he emerged comfortably best of the home team and ought to do well in novice hurdles next season; chased leader, travelled well, shaken up home turn, not quicken early in straight, kept on final 1f. **Blackbow** looked the pick of his stable's quintet on form, but he spoilt his chance by pulling for so long, still not settled down the hill, his chance surely compromised; waited with, refused to settle, effort approaching straight, not quicken over 1f out; he has the physique for jumping. **Felix Desjy** in first-time hood after 4 months off, confirmed himself a useful performer in this sphere under a change of tactics, though he'd have surely done better had he settled at all, going strongly turning for home but having used up too much energy to last home; held up, pulled hard, smooth headway home turn, second early in straight, ridden over 1f out, found little; has the potential to do well over jumps, if his exuberance can be channelled correctly. **Colreevy** progressed again, having come from a similar position to the winner but, after travelling rather better, not finishing off the race anything like so well; dropped out, travelled well, steady headway 4f out, ridden straight, one paced over 1f out. **Mercy Mercy Me** after 4 months off, built on debut promise in this significantly higher grade, still in need of experience; dropped out, took keen hold, headway over 4f out, shaken up entering straight, hung left, not quicken over 1f out; a scopey sort, he's open to further improvement and will have a bright future over jumps. **Rhinestone** was below the form he showed last time, finding this too much of a test of stamina; in touch, chased leaders approaching straight, weakened over 1f out; he's not much on looks compared to most of these. **Didtheyleaveuoutto** was towards the head of the list in terms of what had been achieved already, but he wasn't in the same form as at Ascot, softer ground possibly a factor, alongside the winner early in the straight but unable to finish to anything like the same effect; held up, headway 3f out, ridden straight, not quicken over 1f out. **The Big Bite** had achieved more than most of the home team and might have been expected to do better, not helping his cause by failing to settle; held up, not settle fully, shaken up over 3f out, carried head bit awkwardly, made little impression; he was one of the better types and should have a future over jumps. **Seddon** up in grade, shaped well, looking a threat down the hill before his lack of experience told; held up, travelled well, good progress over 3f out, ridden straight, no extra; remains with potential. **Dashel Drasher** hadn't won much of a race at Wincanton and ran about as well as could have been expected upped in grade; chased leaders, ridden 4f out, left behind home turn; he isn't at all a bad type and could well have a future over jumps. **Know The Score** was one of the more prominent British-trained runners in the betting, but this was asking a lot after his debut success in a small field and he wasn't up to the task, albeit shaping better than the distance beaten suggests; prominent, shaken up over 3f out, weakened over 1f out, not knocked about. **Arch My Boy** ran about as well as could have been expected upped in grade, just not competitive; held up, effort 4f out, some headway home turn, one paced. **Stoney Mountain** one of the lesser types in appearance, was found out in significantly better company, in trouble a good way out; mid-division, effort when met some trouble end of back straight, left behind soon after. **Jaytrack Parkhomes** was attempting to follow Cue Card, in landing this as a 4-y-o after a debut success at Fontwell, but he couldn't get close to emulating his stable-companion; in touch, ridden 4f out, left behind before straight. **Volcano** was well held on first outing since leaving Christian Williams after 10 weeks off, beaten by more than the longer trip; mid-division, labouring over 4f out; he beat Acey Milan on debut but hasn't gone on from that. **Nestor Park** was very unlikely to make an impact at this level and finished well held, though he shaped a bit better than the distances suggest; handy, travelled well, shaken up 3f out, weakened approaching straight; he has a bit about him physically and ought to make an impact at an ordinary level once over jumps. **The Flying Sofa** had a lot more on here than previously and just wasn't up to the task; handy, took keen hold, ridden 4f out, soon done with. **Doc Penfro** has scope and may be of interest when sent jumping at a realistic level, but he had no business in this; mid-division, left behind 4f out. **Crooks Peak** last seen winning the listed bumper here in November, ran no sort of race after 4 months off, clearly not himself; mid-division, left behind over 4f out, tailed off straight. **Thebannerkingrebel** unbeaten in 2 starts, had a fair bit more on in this company but plainly didn't give his running regardless; in rear, labouring over 5f out, pulled up over 1f out.

CHELTENHAM Thursday March 15
SOFT

JLT Novices' Chase (Golden Miller) (Grade 1) (1)

Pos	Btn	Horse	Age	Wgt	Eq	Trainer	Jockey	SP
1		SHATTERED LOVE (IRE)	7	10-11	(t)	Gordon Elliott, Ireland	J. W. Kennedy	4/1
2	7	TERREFORT (FR)	5	11-3		Nicky Henderson	Daryl Jacob	3/1f
3	5	BENATAR (IRE)	6	11-4		Gary Moore	Jamie Moore	10/1
4	2½	KEMBOY (FR)	6	11-4		W. P. Mullins, Ireland	D. J. Mullins	15/2
5	¾	FINIAN'S OSCAR (IRE)	6	11-4	(s+t)	Colin Tizzard	Robbie Power	11/2
6	6	WEST APPROACH	8	11-4	(b)	Colin Tizzard	Tom Scudamore	33/1
7	4	BIGMARTRE (FR)	7	11-4		Harry Whittington	Harry Bannister	20/1
8	14	MODUS	8	11-4		Paul Nicholls	Barry Geraghty	12/1
pu		INVITATION ONLY (IRE)	7	11-4		W. P. Mullins, Ireland	P. Townend	9/2

9 ran   Race Time 5m 12.20   Closing Sectional (4.0f): 58.3s (107.6%)   Winning Owner: Gigginstown House Stud

There perhaps wasn't the depth to this that there might have been, but the first 2 had already won at Grade 1 level, and there's no reason to think the runner-up didn't give his running, the winner the first mare to land a novice chase at the Festival since Brief Gale won the RSA in 1995; jumping was an issue with a few of the also-rans, 1 or 2 unlikely ever to fully deliver on their ability as a result, though both Kemboy and Invitation Only remain with potential. **Shattered Love** all at sea on good ground in the Baring Bingham last season, had taken her form to a different level over fences and, with the ground in her favour this time, became the first mare to win a novice chase at the meeting in 23 years, going one better than Ms Parfois on the first day, well backed to do so; in touch, jumped soundly, travelled well, headway 3 out, hung left straight, led soon after 2 out, jinked run-in, kept on well; she overcame the drop in trip rather than benefited from it, and there is likely to be more to come when she returns to 3m, clearly thriving, a rematch with Presenting Percy at Punchestown one to savour, though it remains to be seen how crucial soft ground is with her. **Terrefort** fully confirmed the form he'd shown at Sandown, the third successive winner of the Scilly Isles to finish runner-up here, the concession of 7 lb to the winner just beyond him; close up, travelled well, led after 3 out, quickened entering straight, headed soon after 2 out, kept on, no match for winner; he's only a 5-y-o, with only 3 runs for this yard, and should continue to thrive for a while yet. **Benatar** lost his unbeaten record over fences, not helping his cause by racing so freely after 12 weeks off; in touch, took very strong hold, effort 3 out, not quicken, mistake last, rallied to take third final 100 yds, finished lame. **Kemboy** well backed, ran creditably upped in grade, under a change of tactics, likely to have done even better had he not rooted the first ditch; held up, bad mistake ninth, shaken up 4 out, some headway entering straight, faded run-in; remains open to improvement. **Finian's Oscar** back over fences, doesn't really convince as a chaser, despite his physique, and he ran no more than respectably in first-time cheekpieces, again not finishing his race that well either; chased leaders, mistake ninth, loomed up 3 out, not fluent there, soon done with. **West Approach** ran respectably in first-time blinkers, though no better, his season over fences not having progressed in the way that looked likely early on; held up, labouring twelfth, weakening when mistake 2 out. **Bigmartre** was worth a try up in trip, but the grade proved beyond him, left behind in the closing stages, still early days, though, and likely to make an impact back in handicaps; led, jumped right at times, shaken up 4 out, headed after 3 out, weakened straight. **Modus** back under more usual tactics in a serious race, was easy to back and well held, his jumping just not cutting the mustard; waited with, took keen hold, bad mistake tenth, blundered 4 out, labouring after; he's probably not going to be easy to place. **Invitation Only** had leading form claims, but didn't get the chance to show what he could do, effectively out of the race at the top of the hill; held up, travelled well, yet to be asked for effort when all but came down 4 out and pulled up; he remains open to improvement.

Ryanair Chase (Festival Trophy) (Grade 1) (1)

Pos	Btn	Horse	Age	Wgt	Eq	Trainer	Jockey	SP
1		BALKO DES FLOS (FR)	7	11-10		Henry de Bromhead, Ireland	Davy Russell	8/1
2	4½	UN DE SCEAUX (FR)	10	11-10		W. P. Mullins, Ireland	P. Townend	8/11f
3	8	CLOUDY DREAM (IRE)	8	11-10		Ruth Jefferson	Brian Hughes	10/1
4	15	SUB LIEUTENANT (IRE)	9	11-10	(t)	Henry de Bromhead, Ireland	Sean Flanagan	18/1
5	9	FRODON (FR)	6	11-10	(t)	Paul Nicholls	Sam Twiston-Davies	9/1
pu		CUE CARD	12	11-10	(t)	Colin Tizzard	Paddy Brennan	9/2

6 ran Race Time 5m 23.20 Closing Sectional (4.0f): 61.7s (101.0%) Winning Owner: Gigginstown House Stud

The smallest field in the history of the Festival Trophy, since it replaced the Cathcart in 2005, and a rather disappointing contest, neither of the previous winners in the field seeming at their best, the winner perhaps not needing to improve all that much to gain a first success at this level, the first also for the sponsor in a race carrying its present name since the second running. **Balko des Flos** had seemed to excel himself when a 66/1-chance at Leopardstown last time, but more than confirmed that form, under a more patient ride, back on softer going and back down in trip, though there is a suspicion that he was the only one at his best; waited with, travelled well, headway 4 out, led on bridle 3 out, kicked on entering straight, shaken up before last, not fluent there, ridden out; either Aintree or Punchestown would provide an opportunity to confirm whether he's going to be a player in stronger races at this level. **Un de Sceaux** bidding for a third Festival win, having also been second to Sprinter Sacre in the 2016 Champion Chase, looked to have plenty going for him but he wasn't able to produce his best, capitulating pretty tamely in the straight; prominent, took strong hold, led fifth, clear tenth, reduced advantage 4 out, headed next, not quicken entering straight; he'd faced simple tasks on his first 2 starts of the campaign and it may be time is catching up with him at the highest level. **Cloudy Dream** seemed likely to benefit from the drop back down in trip, but his jumping was a little below its usual standard and he never landed a blow in a race in which he needed to improve to get involved in any case; patiently ridden, not always fluent, travelled well, crept closer after 4 out, third straight, mistake 2 out, no extra. **Sub Lieutenant** had chased home Un de Sceaux in last season's renewal, but just wasn't in the same form this time round, after 3 months off; chased leader until sixth, not fluent seventh, labouring 4 out; he holds a Grand National entry, but lack of stamina would surely be a major concern. **Frodon** had put up a performance when winning here in January that justified him taking his chance, but he's not reproduced that improvement in 2 starts since, well held this time, extreme ground and a very good ride showing him to optimum advantage that day; held up, labouring thirteenth. **Cue Card** clearly wasn't himself, perhaps his race left at Ascot, wisely pulled up when it was clear he was just not going, a low-key swansong to a Cheltenham career that began with a win in the 2010 Champion Bumper.

Sun Bets Stayers' Hurdle (Grade 1) (1)

Pos	Btn	Horse	Age	Wgt	Eq	Trainer	Jockey	SP
1		PENHILL	7	11-10		W. P. Mullins, Ireland	P. Townend	12/1
2	2	SUPASUNDAE	8	11-10		Mrs J. Harrington, Ireland	Robbie Power	6/1
3	3	WHOLESTONE (IRE)	7	11-10		Nigel Twiston-Davies	Aidan Coleman	14/1
4	1	COLIN'S SISTER	7	11-3		Fergal O'Brien	Paddy Brennan	33/1
5	nk	SAM SPINNER	6	11-10		Jedd O'Keeffe	Joe Colliver	9/4f
6	½	YANWORTH	8	11-10		Alan King	Barry Geraghty	6/1
7	¾	THE WORLDS END (IRE)	7	11-10		Tom George	A. P. Heskin	33/1
8	½	L'AMI SERGE (IRE)	8	11-10	(h)	Nicky Henderson	Daryl Jacob	14/1
9	6	AUGUSTA KATE	7	11-3		W. P. Mullins, Ireland	D. J. Mullins	20/1
10	1¾	UNOWHATIMEANHARRY	10	11-10	(t)	Harry Fry	Noel Fehily	8/1
11	2¼	DONNA'S DIAMOND (IRE)	9	11-10		Chris Grant	Callum Bewley	66/1
12	hd	THE NEW ONE (IRE)	10	11-10		Nigel Twiston-Davies	Sam Twiston-Davies	18/1
13	1	LIL ROCKERFELLER (USA)	7	11-10	(s)	Neil King	Trevor Whelan	33/1
F		LET'S DANCE (FR)	6	11-3	(s)	W. P. Mullins, Ireland	D. E. Mullins	33/1
F		BACARDYS (FR)	7	11-10		W. P. Mullins, Ireland	Mr P. W. Mullins	14/1

15 ran Race Time 6m 20.50 Closing Sectional (3.7f): 52.9s (111.0%) Winning Owner: Mr Tony Bloom

Despite the large field, the joint biggest in the last decade, there were some notable absentees—the Cleeve winner Agrapart, missing in the expectation of good ground, victors in the Galmoy, Presenting Percy, and Christmas Hurdle, Apple's Jade, who'd both run earlier at the meeting, and the Long Distance Hurdle winner Beer Goggles to name 4—and for one reason the last-named in particular was missed, because he would surely have helped ensure the race was more truly run than it was, the pace surprisingly sedate, given the way Sam Spinner had won at both Haydock and Aintree, the field well bunched 2 out, space at a premium as the tempo finally lifted, speed favoured over stamina, the well-ridden winner, brought wide and out of trouble, and the third filling the same placings they occupied in a steadily-run Spa Hurdle in 2017, the runner-up a Grade 1 winner at 2m last time out; Sam Spinner is top of the list of those unsuited by the way the race was run, though he wasn't alone, some of the riders on others surely guilty of assuming he'd set a good pace, Bacardys among those finding trouble; all in all, the race did little to sort the pecking order in this division, the form best viewed with a degree of caution. **Penhill** didn't have the anticipated Flat campaign last year (reportedly not easy to train) and was running for the first time since Punchestown, but was clearly spot on for the day and, as in the Spa last season, had a race that played to his strengths, aided by a good ride, produced wide to avoid trouble as the field bustled to get a position turning for home; in rear, travelled well, ran wide approaching 2 out, smooth headway soon after, led before last, asserted final 50 yds; he's clearly a high-class staying hurdler, though there are plenty of others with claims to being the best in the division. **Supasundae** running in this in preference to the Champion Hurdle, despite showing improved form in the Irish Champion last time out, had a race that played to his strengths back at 3m and to a large extent confirmed that improvement, though beaten fair and square on the day; mid-division, travelled well, headway 2 out, every chance last, kept on, held final 50 yds; he was runner-up in the Liverpool Hurdle last season, that among the options for him next. **Wholestone** ran up to his best, on a track where he has such a solid record, probably helped more than most by the run of the race, for all that he lacked the pace of the first 2; mid-division, effort 2 out, not quicken before last, kept on well final 1f, took third final 50 yds. **Colin's Sister** ran up to her best, getting going just too late, behind Wholestone for the third start running and really of established merit now; held up, still plenty to do early in straight, kept on well after last, nearest at the finish. **Sam Spinner** strong in the betting, looked the pick on form after his Long Walk win, but he wasn't seen to best advantage, not setting a strong enough pace to bring his stamina and guts into play, his jumping not so good as it had been at Ascot; dictated, tried to quicken after 2 out, shaken up straight, headed before last, not quicken; he is likely to be much better suited by Aintree and could well be the one to beat if sent for the Liverpool Hurdle. **Yanworth** thoroughly unconvincing over fences, despite 2 wins from 4 starts, was here in preference to running in the Golden Miller, at 3m for only the second time (won the Liverpool Hurdle last spring), not disgraced but underwhelming under pressure after being well positioned and in a race that ought to have suited him better than others; prominent, ridden straight, hung left, not quicken; he's come up short at the last 3 Festivals and for all his wins and good strike rate, he's a hard horse to like. **The Worlds End** got back on track to a large extent, his form short of what was required at this level, a switch to fences surely on the cards for next season; held up, effort entering straight, not quicken approaching last. **L'Ami Serge** wasn't disgraced, though given he was second in the County Hurdle in 2017, he might have been expected to do better in a race favouring speed, just not finding up the hill under testing conditions; in rear, headway early in straight, faded after last, never landed a blow. **Augusta Kate** ran close to her best, a shade better than the result after being short of room when making her effort, though her record suggests she was one of the more likely to benefit from the lack of pace and still essentially wasn't good enough; held up, effort after 2 out, met some trouble home turn, not quicken straight. **Unowhatimeanharry** beaten at odds on in this last season and defeated at short odds on his last 2 starts, had been rejected by Geraghty this time and was again a bit below form, though he was another for whom the lack of pace was no use at all; in touch, ridden 2 out, outpaced straight; he bounced back from defeat last season to win at Punchestown, so probably shouldn't be written off if he turns up there or at Aintree. **Donna's Diamond** looked to face a stiff task in this grade and ran as well as could be expected, though it was indicative of the lack of pace that he was still bang there on the bridle at the second last; close up, every chance 2 out, left behind home turn. **The New One** finally tried at 3m, possibly didn't stay, though a more passive ride than usual is unlikely to have done him any favours; handy, ridden after 2 out, weakened approaching last; he's a standing dish in the Aintree Hurdle (won it in 2014) and will presumably run in that, rather than the Liverpool Hurdle next. **Lil Rockerfeller** a gallant second 12 months previously, wasn't in the same form this time round, the run of the race no use to him; prominent, outpaced after 2 out, held when badly hampered last. **Let's Dance** in first-time cheekpieces after her poor effort last time, didn't get far enough to see what effect they would have; held up, fell ninth. **Bacardys** back over hurdles, after 11 weeks off (had missed a run in the Galmoy), looked an interesting runner upped in trip, but didn't get the chance to show all he could do, poorly placed behind horses when the tempo picked up, nevertheless likely to have finished third had he completed; held up, travelled well, looking for a run home turn, good headway when fell last; remains with potential in staying hurdles and one to be interested in if he turns up at Aintree or Punchestown.

CHELTENHAM Friday March 16
HEAVY

JCB Triumph Hurdle (Grade 1) (1)

Pos	Btn	Horse	Age	Wgt	Eq	Trainer	Jockey	SP
1		FARCLAS (FR)	4	11-0	(t)	Gordon Elliott, Ireland	J. W. Kennedy	9/1
2	1¾	MR ADJUDICATOR	4	11-0		W. P. Mullins, Ireland	P. Townend	8/1
3	3½	SAYO	4	11-0		W. P. Mullins, Ireland	D. E. Mullins	33/1
4	1½	APPLE'S SHAKIRA (FR)	4	10-7		Nicky Henderson	Barry Geraghty	6/5f
5	18	SALDIER (FR)	4	11-0		W. P. Mullins, Ireland	D. J. Mullins	14/1
6	2	REDICEAN	4	11-0		Alan King	Wayne Hutchinson	7/1
7	36	SUSSEX RANGER (USA)	4	11-0		Gary Moore	Jamie Moore	28/1
F		STORMY IRELAND (FR)	4	10-7		W. P. Mullins, Ireland	Noel Fehily	9/2
pu		GUMBALL (FR)	4	11-0	(t)	Philip Hobbs	Richard Johnson	40/1

9 ran   Race Time 4m 17.00   Closing Sectional (3.7f): 54.4s (104.0%)   Winning Owner: Gigginstown House Stud

A smaller field Triumph Hurdle than usual and it was was reminiscent of much of the 2018 Festival as Gordon Elliott and Willie Mullins-trained horses dominated, filling the places, and it was the same 1-2 as in the Spring Juvenile at Leopardstown last month; recent winners of this race have struggled to make the step up to open company the following season but this year's winner is rated as high as any bar Peace And Co in the last 5 years. **Farclas** had the scent of a high-flyer from day one over hurdles, when second in a Grade 2, and he's progressing quickly, off the mark in this sphere with this biggest of wins for a juvenile, turning the tables with Mr Adjudicator from Leopardstown last time when both had pulled clear in a very good time, more of the same here as that pair fought it out from the final flight, a first-time tongue strap perhaps helping Farclas in the finish, not flinching at any stage under a strong drive, his attitude looking a real plus; in touch, travelled well, close up when forced to switch between last 2, led approaching last, kept on gamely; there's more improvement to come and he'll stay 2½m. **Mr Adjudicator** wasn't able to beat Farclas again but that rival is just progressing rapidly and he improved further himself still; dropped out, headway when not clear run soon after 2 out, challenged approaching last, one paced final 100 yds; he's hardly the most stoutly bred, a rare National Hunt horse for his sire Camacho, and it wouldn't be a surprise if less testing ground than he's encountered so far over hurdles actually suited for all that he obviously handles these conditions well enough. **Sayo** is clearly reaping the benefit of the Mullins treatment, this just his second start for the yard and showing much improved form to be Grade-1 placed 6 weeks after winning an ordinary maiden hurdle; prominent, went with enthusiasm, not fluent 3 out, not quicken before last, left in a place there, kept on; he had every chance and there's no obvious reason why he should turn the tables with the first 2 in other big juvenile races this spring, but he'll be competitive again. **Apple's Shakira** failed to meet high expectations, very strong in the market right up to the off, but it was respectable effort in by far the deepest race she's been involved in yet and she just seemed a bit raw when asked to work harder than she had before, crucially caught flat-footed turning in; in touch, raced freely, went handy after 3 out, outpaced home turn, held when left in frame last, stayed on again final 100 yds; she's always given the impression that longer trips would ultimately suit and the way she shaped here hammers that home, ready for a step up and still with potential for 2½m+. **Saldier** was found out in better company, not ready for it, but he should still improve another day; held up, mistakes fourth, fifth, some headway 2 out, tied up before last. **Redicean** is better than this and seemed unsuited by the more testing conditions, whilst maybe the fact the Adonis was less than 3 weeks ago worked against him too, turned out quicker than any of his rivals; held up, typically travelled well, yet to be asked for effort when hit 2 out, found little, unsuited by the emphasis on stamina; he can be expected to fare better in the Anniversary at Aintree. **Sussex Ranger** proved to be a disappointment for all that this was a stiff task, very laboured; prominent, not always fluent, off the bridle long way out, struggling when hit 2 out, soon done with. **Stormy Ireland** ran a big race considering how fresh she was, soon pulling her way to the front, still held together on the home turn but headed approaching the last and held in third when taking a tired fall at the final flight; she has some growing up to do still but posesses plenty of ability and remains with potential. **Gumball** might have a physical problem, tongue tied here and seeming amiss; in touch, lost place before 2 out, folded tamely, pulled up before last.

Albert Bartlett Novices' Hurdle (Spa) (Grade 1) (1)

Pos	Btn	Horse	Age	Wgt	Eq	Trainer	Jockey	SP
1		KILBRICKEN STORM (IRE)	7	11-5	(t)	Colin Tizzard	Harry Cobden	33/1
2	3	OK CORRAL (IRE)	8	11-5		Nicky Henderson	Barry Geraghty	16/1
3	1½	SANTINI	6	11-5		Nicky Henderson	Nico de Boinville	11/4f
4	1½	BALLYWARD (IRE)	6	11-5		W. P. Mullins, Ireland	P. Townend	20/1
5	1¾	TOWER BRIDGE (IRE)	5	11-5	(t)	Joseph Patrick O'Brien, Ireland	J. J. Slevin	33/1
6	2¾	ROBIN WATERS (FR)	5	11-5		Dan Skelton	Harry Skelton	50/1
7	1¼	FABULOUS SAGA (FR)	6	11-5	(t)	W. P. Mullins, Ireland	D. E. Mullins	20/1
8	14	DORTMUND PARK (FR)	5	11-5	(t)	Gordon Elliott, Ireland	Davy Russell	12/1
9	13	CHRIS'S DREAM (IRE)	6	11-5		Henry de Bromhead, Ireland	Mark Walsh	6/1
10	2¾	POETIC RHYTHM (IRE)	7	11-5		Fergal O'Brien	Paddy Brennan	10/1
11	9	REAL STEEL (FR)	5	11-5		W. P. Mullins, Ireland	D. J. Mullins	33/1
12	3	ENNISCOFFEY OSCAR (IRE)	6	11-5		Emma Lavelle	Leighton Aspell	25/1
13	hd	PAISLEY PARK (IRE)	6	11-5	(v)	Emma Lavelle	Nick Scholfield	33/1
pu		BEYOND THE LAW (IRE)	6	11-5	(t)	M. F. Morris, Ireland	Robbie Power	50/1
pu		CALETT MAD (FR)	6	11-5	(t)	Nigel Twiston-Davies	Daryl Jacob	16/1
pu		CHEF DES OBEAUX (FR)	6	11-5		Nicky Henderson	Noel Fehily	6/1
pu		CRUCIAL ROLE	6	11-5		Henry Daly	Richard Johnson	66/1
pu		MR WHIPPED (IRE)	5	11-5		Nicky Henderson	Jeremiah McGrath	16/1
pu		MULCAHYS HILL (IRE)	6	11-5		Warren Greatrex	A. P. Heskin	50/1
pu		TALKISCHEAP (IRE)	6	11-5		Alan King	Wayne Hutchinson	25/1

20 ran Race Time 6m 13.70 Closing Sectional (3.7f): 58.9s (97.9%) Winning Owner: A Selway & P Wavish

Very testing ground and a strong gallop made this an even more thorough test of stamina than usual and, to put things into context, the race time was over 24 seconds slower than when Penhill won in 2017; because of the different test it was a different type of horse that came to the fore, suiting the stoutly-bred staying chasers of the future, a description that fits most of the principals. **Kilbricken Storm** could be excused a below-par run in the Challow (turned out too quickly) and, having been freshened up by an 11-week break since, he got back on the up under conditions that he'd already proven himself when winning a C&D Grade 2 in December; tracked pace, travelled well, chased leader before 2 out, led approaching last, hung left, as he has before, but kept going well; he's unbeaten over 3m and will probably go to Aintree for the Sefton, though whether that track and the likely better ground will suit him quite so well is doubtful. **Ok Corral** is really showing his talent now, better with every hurdles start, up in trip and grade here and coping on both scores, arguably shaping like the best horse in the race but just costing himself by not immediately knuckling down for pressure; mid-division, travelled strongly, good progress soon after 2 out, hung badly left approaching last and blundered there, then stayed on in the final 100 yds and still closing the gap on the winner at the line; he's the oldest in this field, aged 8, but remains low mileage, should make a chaser and seems to be standing up well to training/racing now (open to further improvement). **Santini** is as good a long-term chasing prospect as there is in the field, a point winner with a strong physique, and his defeat of Ballymore runner-up Black Op in an excellent relative time here in January clearly reads very well, inexperience perhaps a factor in his defeat in this bigger field, although he hardly got the ideal ride either, taken widest of all virtually throughout; raced off the pace, went in snatches, headway before 2 out, took third run-in, kept on well; stamina for this longer trip certainly wasn't a problem and he'll stay even longer distances when he goes over fences, one to follow in that sphere next season. **Ballyward** was up markedly in class after winning a maiden just 6 weeks earlier but coped well with that and relished the 4f longer trip; dropped out, headway between 3 out and 2 out, still plenty to do home turn, stayed on, suited by emphasis on stamina; he will stay long distances and is a cracking chasing prospect, whilst there's probably better still to come in this sphere too. **Tower Bridge** ran at least as well in defeat as when winning a weaker Grade 1 the time before, not having a problem with the 2f longer trip; held up, headway before 2 out, outpaced home turn, held when mistake last, kept on. **Robin Waters** is at an earlier stage in his development than most of those that beat him, not only very lightly raced but just a 5-y-o too, and this was a good effort up in grade, promising even more with how he went through the race, not such a strong stayer at 3m under these testing conditions at this stage; mid-division, travelled well, chased leaders before 2 out, not fluent last, no extra; he's a promising young horse who'll go on to better things. **Fabulous Saga** ran up to his previous form whilst shaping much better than the distance beaten suggests; forced pace, travelled strongly, headed seventh, led again 3 out, clear home turn but started to tie up and headed approaching the last, finishing tired having done too much too soon; he's won twice over 3m but doesn't lack pace. **Dortmund Park** wasn't up to the task, found out in Grade 1's the last twice, but he could be a better chaser in the future and should stay 3m; in rear, took closer order 3 out, outpaced approaching 2 out. **Chris's Dream** wasn't that easy to assess after such a dominant display in a small field last time and found this too much; close up, led seventh, headed 3 out, weakened between last 2. **Poetic Rhythm** had the winner behind when winning the Challow but didn't give his running 11 weeks on; chased leaders, weakened after 2 out, eased off; there was more to this than lack of stamina and he should prove effective at 3m another day. **Real Steel** had only run at around 2m before and probably didn't relish such a slog up, struggling before 2 out and always behind. **Enniscoffey Oscar** was possibly unsuited by conditions that were even more testing than he'd won under at Doncaster last time and never landed a blow. **Paisley Park** ran no sort of race in first-time visor, perhaps not facing it; raced off the pace, went in snatches, behind from 5 out. **Beyond The Law** who'd had a wind operation since his last start, was out of his depth; chased leaders, lost place after 3 out, pulled up before next. **Calett Mad** is useful on his day but hasn't always fired this season and this wasn't a going day; mid-division, lost place after sixth, tailed off when pulled up before last. **Chef des Obeaux** had been so progressive and clearly wasn't 100% this day; held up, in touch 3 out, weakened between last 2, pulled up, seemed amiss. **Crucial Role** found this too competitive; mid-division, mid-race mistakes, struggling badly after 3 out, pulled up. **Mr Whipped** was held but still in eighth position, running some sort of race, when pulled up before the last, something possibly amiss with him, though given he was out of the prize money it's also possible his rider just wanted to spare him a hard race. **Mulcahys Hill** ran no sort of race, disappointing since the Challow; chased leaders, off the bridle long way out, lost touch 3 out, pulled up before next. **Talkischeap** wasn't up to this better company; mid-division, struggling badly before 3 out, tailed off when pulled up.

Timico Cheltenham Gold Cup Chase (Grade 1) (1)

Pos	Btn	Horse	Age	Wgt	Eq	Trainer	Jockey	SP
1		NATIVE RIVER (IRE)	8	11-10	(s)	Colin Tizzard	Richard Johnson	5/1
2	4½	MIGHT BITE (IRE)	9	11-10		Nicky Henderson	Nico de Boinville	4/1f
3	4	ANIBALE FLY (FR)	8	11-10	(t)	A. J. Martin, Ireland	Barry Geraghty	33/1
4	4	ROAD TO RESPECT (IRE)	7	11-10	(h)	Noel Meade, Ireland	Sean Flanagan	9/1
5	8	DJAKADAM (FR)	9	11-10		W. P. Mullins, Ireland	Mr P. W. Mullins	25/1
6	18	DEFINITLY RED (IRE)	9	11-10		Brian Ellison	Danny Cook	8/1
7	1½	TEA FOR TWO	9	11-10		Nick Williams	Lizzie Kelly	50/1
8	7	EDWULF	9	11-10	(t)	Joseph Patrick O'Brien, Ireland	Mr Derek O'Connor	20/1
9	18	AMERICAN (FR)	8	11-10		Harry Fry	Noel Fehily	25/1
F		BACHASSON (FR)	7	11-10		W. P. Mullins, Ireland	D. E. Mullins	33/1
F		TOTAL RECALL (IRE)	9	11-10		W. P. Mullins, Ireland	D. J. Mullins	14/1
pu		KILLULTAGH VIC (IRE)	9	11-10		W. P. Mullins, Ireland	P. Townend	8/1
pu		OUR DUKE (IRE)	8	11-10		Mrs J. Harrington, Ireland	Robbie Power	9/2
pu		OUTLANDER (IRE)	10	11-10	(s)	Gordon Elliott, Ireland	J. W. Kennedy	20/1
pu		SAPHIR DU RHEU (FR)	9	11-10	(t)	Paul Nicholls	Sam Twiston-Davies	66/1

15 ran Race Time 7m 02.60 Closing Sectional (4f): 60.9s (105.5%) Winning Owner: Brocade Racing

Rewind 10 years and it was Denman vs Kauto Star in a most compelling Gold Cup duel, and although the 2018 renewal of National Hunt racing's most prestigious contest may not have had the same pre-race draw or quite the same level of quality it did develop into an enthralling showdown between 2 of the market leaders, fantastic viewing as Native River and Might Bite went head-to-head from flagfall, admittedly not at a strong early pace, but neither put a foot wrong and piled the pressure on the chasing pack a long way out, with only the odd one of them even threatening to get involved in the battle up ahead; the winner had been third in the race 12 months earlier, behind Sizing John, who was ruled out by injury this time around, whilst Minella Rocco—second in 2017—was pulled out on the day because of worsening ground. **Native River** had a different preparation for this year's Gold Cup, and that he arrived a fresher horse than 12 months earlier was probably a help, his small-field Newbury win the ideal stepping stone to get him here all guns blazing for a career-best performance, whilst conditions were a factor too, bringing his stamina into play more than on good ground last year; forcing the pace, he jumped boldly, ridden after 3 out and headed narrowly 2 out, immediately fighting back and in front again jumping the last, edging right but finding plenty up the hill, outstaying the runner-up; this gave trainer Colin Tizzard a first Gold Cup win and

Champion Jockey Richard Johnson a second 18 years after Looks Like Trouble, and no doubt Native River will be back to make another bold bid in the next couple of years, not over-raced for an 8-y-o which ought to help with his longevity; shorter term he'll probably go for the Bowl at Aintree, where he won the Mildmay as a novice, but a thorough test suits him best and if he comes up against Might Bite again over 1f shorter on the flat track there he's going to be vulnerable to his speed. **Might Bite** is a class act and for 95% of this he looked just that, so impressive with how he kept tabs with Native River, matching him stride for stride and jump for jump, stamina his shortfall in the end on very testing ground over the longest trip he's ever tackled; pressed leader, jumped superbly, travelled strongly, led 2 out, headed last, no extra final 100 yds, outstayed by a stamina-laden rival; he won at Aintree a few weeks after his RSA success last year and the Bowl there next month looks the ideal next race for him as that will place slightly less emphasis on stamina and more on his high-cruising speed and excellent jumping. **Anibale Fly** was very well suited by this thorough stamina test, tackling a longer trip than before, possible he'd have got closer still but for a couple of small errors coming down the hill for the last time, but he ran the race of his life anyway; mid-division, closing when mistake 4 out, hit 3 out, took third last, stayed on well; he'll be an interesting runner if taking his chance in the Grand National as a mark of 159 is lenient on this form and he shapes as if he'll stay extreme distances. **Road To Respect** has come a long way since winning the Plate at this meeting last year, a bona-fide Grade 1 horse now, not quite repeating the form of his Leopardstown win over Christmas but still running with credit to hit the frame on ground that was more testing than he's shown his very best form; mid-division, travelled well, headway sixteenth, went third 4 out, driven before 2 out, not fluent there, one paced; he has time on his side, younger than any of the other principals, and it'd be no surprise at all if he made an even bigger impact in future Gold Cups. **Djakadam** shaped better than the distance beaten suggests, his stamina stretched on ground that was more testing than for the 3 previous Gold Cups he'd contested, whilst some errors wouldn't have helped with his finishing effort either; tracked pace, travelled well, blundered thirteenth, mistakes 5 out, 3 out, no extra between last 2; it's not been his best season but there was more verve about him this day and it's worth remembering that he's run some of his very best races at Punchestown, including when pushing Sizing John close there last April. **Definitly Red** had won Grade 2's the last twice but neither of those are particularly strong pieces of form and he found this too competitive up against the best staying chasers around; chased leaders but always looked uncomfortable with the pace, lost place fifteenth, well off pace after next, merely plugged on. **Tea For Two** completed 12 months on from an early unseat in this race but never threatened to get seriously involved from the back of the field on ground that was more testing than his optimum; he ought to run much better in the Bowl at Aintree, a race he won in 2017. **Edwulf** showed last time that he can produce a top-class performance but couldn't get close to repeating that effort 6 weeks on; in rear, some headway 4 out, weakened after next. **American** didn't disgrace himself, in the mix for a long way, but quite simply wasn't up to the task; chased leaders, lost place 4 out, beaten next, weakened. **Bachasson** fell at the second. **Total Recall** faced his toughest task yet but has had a progressive campaign and was in the process of running well when departing; held up, headway 5 out, ridden after

4 out, keeping on when fell next, in sixth place and only around a length behind Anibale Fly at the time; he got straight up and galloped away and, though it's hardly ideal to go into a Grand National on the back of a fall, he still appeals as well handicapped (BHA-rated 156) and that's reportedly been his main target since winning the Ladbrokes Trophy in the autumn. **Killultagh Vic** was let down by jumping 5 weeks after a crunching fall in the Irish Gold Cup, struggling badly 5 out and pulled up between last 2 having not made an impression. **Our Duke** didn't cope with this most demanding of examinations, his suspect jumping failing to pass muster, though the way he stopped pointed towards a physical issue as well; chased leaders, jumped sketchily, blundered thirteenth, never going well after, stopped quickly after sixteenth, pulled up before 4 out. **Outlander** is prone to poor runs and this was one of them, yet to fire in this race after 2 tries; held up, labouring seventeenth, lost touch after 4 out, not keen on the day and pulled up between the last 2. **Saphir du Rheu** was fifth in last year's Gold Cup but has had problems since (now tongue tied) and went backwards from his reappearance; raced wide, mid-division, lost touch after sixteenth, pulled up before 4 out; he's plenty to prove now.

AINTREE Thursday April 12
SOFT

Betway Bowl Chase (Grade 1) (1)

Pos	Btn	Horse	Age	Wgt	Eq	Trainer	Jockey	SP
1		MIGHT BITE (IRE)	9	11-7		Nicky Henderson	Nico de Boinville	4/5f
2	7	BRISTOL DE MAI (FR)	7	11-7		Nigel Twiston-Davies	Daryl Jacob	5/1
3	3¼	CLAN DES OBEAUX (FR)	6	11-7		Paul Nicholls	Harry Cobden	8/1
4	3	SIZING CODELCO (IRE)	9	11-7		Colin Tizzard	Robbie Power	33/1
5	¾	SUB LIEUTENANT (IRE)	9	11-7	(t)	Henry de Bromhead, Ireland	Sean Flanagan	25/1
6	23	TEA FOR TWO	9	11-7		Nick Williams	Lizzie Kelly	12/1
7	3	DOUBLE SHUFFLE (IRE)	8	11-7	(h)	Tom George	A. P. Heskin	11/1
ur		DEFINITLY RED (IRE)	9	11-7		Brian Ellison	Danny Cook	8/1

8 ran Race Time 6m 39.30 Closing Sectional (3.15f): 48.8s (103.3%) Winning Owner: The Knot Again Partnership

This was envisaged as a Gold Cup consolation race when the current pattern was first formed and, even though these days it has the same grading—if not status—as the blue riband itself, it continues to act in that original role, Might Bite following such as Cue Card and Silviniaco Conti in gaining some recompense for a Cheltenham reverse; with 2 runners with a Grade 1 victory to their name this season dominating virtually throughout, the race was a joy to watch, even if not quite so gripping as the Gold Cup, as in the King George Might Bite never really looking in danger of defeat, his performance among the best in this race in recent years, the third shaping encouragingly on a first try at this level, the fourth and fifth never involved and probably flattered. **Might Bite** was clearly none the worse for his exertions at Cheltenham and produced a sparkling display, as good as any he's produced over fences, his jumping a joy to behold (slight mistake 4 out notwithstanding); close up, jumped really well in main, tanked along, disputed lead briefly tenth, pressed leader again fifteenth, went on 3 out, in command approaching last, ridden out; good staying chasers are fragile things, but fingers crossed that he can have another full campaign at the top level, with the £1m bonus for winning at Haydock, Kempton and Cheltenham reportedly the aim next season. **Bristol de Mai** got back on track after 2 disappointing efforts, making a much better fist of things than he had against Might Bite in the King

George, just outclassed by a better rival; led, joined briefly tenth, joined again fifteenth, left behind by winner from 3 out; he'll presumably be trained for Wetherby and, particularly, Haydock in mind in the autumn, the latter his best chance of gaining a verdict over the winner. **Clan des Obeaux** ran well after 4 months off over 3f longer trip, opening up options for next season, the youngest of these and still with untapped potential; in touch, hampered before ninth, effort straight, kept on. **Sizing Codelco** seemed to run very well up in grade, though it was hardly the performance of a horse suddenly in top form, never really travelling and jumping indifferently, likely to be flattered; in rear, jumped none too fluently, soon off bridle, headway early in straight, stayed on. **Sub Lieutenant** appeared to run up to his season's best, back at around 3m, though, rather like the fourth, he just closed up late on and may be flattered; held up, labouring fourteenth, tailed off early in straight, stayed on late on. **Tea For Two** was unable to repeat his heroics of 12 months previously, finishing well held; held up, ridden straight, weakened after 3 out. **Double Shuffle** ran poorly after 4 months off, seemingly unsettled by a couple of mistakes on the final circuit; in touch, mistake twelfth, off the bridle when mistake fourteenth, soon labouring. **Definitly Red** didn't get very far; prominent, bad mistake and unseated rider third.

Betway Aintree Hurdle (Grade 1) (1)

Pos	Btn	Horse	Age	Wgt	Eq	Trainer	Jockey	SP
1		L'AMI SERGE (IRE)	8	11-7	(h)	Nicky Henderson	Daryl Jacob	5/1
2	3	SUPASUNDAE	8	11-7		Mrs J. Harrington, Ireland	Robbie Power	11/10f
3	3¾	CLYNE	8	11-7		Evan Williams	Adam Wedge	25/1
4	6	MY TENT OR YOURS (IRE)	11	11-7	(h)	Nicky Henderson	Barry Geraghty	9/2
5	9	CYRUS DARIUS	9	11-7		Ruth Jefferson	Brian Hughes	12/1
6	23	DIAKALI (FR)	9	11-7	(b)	Gary Moore	Joshua Moore	25/1
7	46	IZZO (GER)	5	11-7	(h)	Mlle C. Fey, France	Richard Johnson	50/1
pu		AIR HORSE ONE	7	11-7		Harry Fry	Noel Fehily	20/1
pu		THE NEW ONE (IRE)	10	11-7		Nigel Twiston-Davies	Sam Twiston-Davies	8/1

9 ran   Race Time 5m 05.30   Closing Sectional (3.15f): 47.9s (100.4%)   Winning Owner: Mr Simon Munir & Mr Isaac Souede

A more open race than the betting indicated, 4 closely matched on their best form, one of those failing to give their running, the others all in contention before the last, the stoutest stayer of the 3 coming out on top, circumstances perfect for him, Diakali tearing off in front ensuring the main group was racing from a fair way out, the third, who raced a clear second between the leader and the rest probably ridden to optimum advantage and likely to be flattered. **L'Ami Serge** had a race that showed him to maximum advantage, getting a great tow into the race and then outstaying his main rivals after the last, no sign of him shirking the issue at all, that aspect of his character perhaps overblown, defeats on 2 of his first 3 starts in Britain this season more to do with the ride given, nothing wrong with his finishing effort behind Sam Spinner in the Long Walk; held up, travelled well, headway 3 out, switched after 2 out, led soon after last, kept on well, ridden out. **Supasundae** second in the Liverpool Hurdle last season, was dropped back in trip under more testing conditions this time round, but again had to settle for the runner-up's spot, running with credit but beaten by a stouter stayer; patiently ridden, went third fifth, headway before 3 out, ridden next, led briefly last, kept on. **Clyne** seemed to excel himself, though there is a good chance he was flattered, racing clear of the rest and ridden much more efficiently than the leader; not always fluent, raced a clear second, led before 3 out, ridden soon after, headed before last, not quicken; it remains to be seen whether he can back this up. **My Tent Or Yours** who'd been forced to miss the Champion Hurdle, wasn't disgraced after 4 months off, this just too much of a test of stamina; patiently ridden, travelled well, headway before 3 out, ridden next, no extra run-in; he's been a grand servant for connections over many years, playing his part in so many top 2m hurdles, one last hurrah at Punchestown hopefully a higher note on which to bow out. **Cyrus Darius** was below form, up in grade, not quite seeing things out after coming with a promising run in the straight; held up, headway before 3 out, not fluent there, ridden 2 out, beaten when untidy last; he has won at this trip over fences, but his stamina was possibly stretched by this sort of test. **Diakali** was well held on first outing since leaving Willie Mullins after 12 months off, looking fit beforehand but going off much too hard for his own good; soon well clear, reduced advantage after eighth, headed 3 out, weakened quickly. **Izzo** looked terrible beforehand, lean and sweating, though would have been out of his depth even if he'd looked a million dollars; in rear, made mistakes, tailed off straight, nursed home. **Air Horse One** found this much too competitive; held up, not fluent sixth, labouring eighth, tailed off when pulled up next. **The New One** has a fine record in this race, but just wasn't himself, whether unsettled by the tactics of others or something not right; led main group, jumped right, lost third fifth, ridden before eighth, weakened end of back straight, pulled up 3 out.

AINTREE Friday April 13
HEAVY

Betway Mildmay Novices' Chase (Grade 1) (1)

Pos	Btn	Horse	Age	Wgt	Eq	Trainer	Jockey	SP
1		TERREFORT (FR)	5	11-4		Nicky Henderson	Daryl Jacob	3/1f
2	3¾	MS PARFOIS (IRE)	7	10-11	(t)	Anthony Honeyball	Noel Fehily	9/2
3	9	ELEGANT ESCAPE (IRE)	6	11-4	(s)	Colin Tizzard	Harry Cobden	4/1
4	18	BLACK CORTON (FR)	7	11-4	(t)	Paul Nicholls	Bryony Frost	6/1
5	6	CAPTAIN CHAOS (IRE)	7	11-4	(b)	Dan Skelton	Harry Skelton	25/1
6	57	HOGAN'S HEIGHT (IRE)	7	11-4	(t)	Jamie Snowden	Gavin Sheehan	33/1
pu		COO STAR SIVOLA (FR)	6	11-4		Nick Williams	Lizzie Kelly	7/1
pu		SNOW FALCON (IRE)	8	11-4		Noel Meade, Ireland	Sean Flanagan	7/1
pu		TESTIFY (IRE)	7	11-4		Donald McCain	Brian Hughes	16/1

9 ran   Race Time 6m 47.70   Closing Sectional (3.15f): 50.1s (102.7%)   Winning Owner: Mr Simon Munir & Mr Isaac Souede

Probably not the strongest renewal of the Mildmay, though the form amongst the principals at least has a solid look to it, Terrefort becoming the third winner to emerge from the JLT at Cheltenham within 24 hours; the gallop was a stop-start one, yet the several injections of pace by leader Captain Chaos ensured stamina was firmly tested. **Terrefort** has made a splendid start for present connections, coping fine with the step up in trip to take his tally to 3 wins from 4 starts for them; mid-division, jumped well in main (hit fourteenth), travelled smoothly, crept closer from end of back straight, produced to lead approaching last, driven clear (saw things out well); remains capable of better, whilst this clearly opens up options with regards to trip—indeed, it wouldn't be a surprise to see him back here over the National fences at some stage in the future. **Ms Parfois** is ending her campaign in fine heart, running at least as well as at Cheltenham in filling the runner-up spot again; mid-division, jumped fluently, travelled well, produced to lead 3 out, headed approaching last, stayed on; worth another try at long distances and may yet do better granted such a test. **Elegant Escape** ran just respectably in first-time cheekpieces, not helped by a mixed round of jumping; chased leader, mistakes back straight on final circuit, led briefly leaving home turn, rallied from 3 out until one paced approaching last; he's another who'll probably prove best off in long-distance handicaps rather than graded events from now on. **Black Corton** was well held under a change of tactics, seeming unsuited by conditions placing the emphasis so much on stamina; held up, hit first, headway end of back straight, challenged briefly 3 out, weakened from next. **Captain Chaos** faced a stiff task in this grade and was well held under an attacking ride; soon well clear, clouted seventh (not his first error), kicked on early final circuit, blundered again 5 out, headed leaving home turn, soon done with. **Hogan's Height** was out of his depth and is better judged on his recent winning form in a lower grade; soon behind, jumped none too fluently, struggling some way out. **Coo Star Sivola** clearly wasn't 100% on the day, possibly over the top for the season; waited with, normally jumps much better (several mistakes), went rather in snatches, beaten end of back straight. **Snow Falcon** was below form after 11 days off, the manner in which he checked out so tamely suggesting something might have been amiss; mid-division, not always fluent, lost place briefly eighth, in contention end of back straight, folded home turn. **Testify** followed a below-par effort with an even worse one (also ran miserably at this fixture last year); in touch, mid-race mistakes, dropped away from early final circuit, looked none too keen (tended to hang left); questions to answer now.

JLT Melling Chase (Grade 1) (1)

Pos	Btn	Horse	Age	Wgt	Eq	Trainer	Jockey	SP
1		POLITOLOGUE (FR)	7	11-7	(h+t)	Paul Nicholls	Sam Twiston-Davies	11/1
2	nk	MIN (FR)	7	11-7		W. P. Mullins, Ireland	P. Townend	11/10f
3	20	SIZING GRANITE (IRE)	10	11-7	(t)	Colin Tizzard	Robbie Power	20/1
4	13	BALKO DES FLOS (FR)	7	11-7		Henry de Bromhead, Ireland	Davy Russell	2/1
5	8	CLOUDY DREAM (IRE)	8	11-7		Ruth Jefferson	Brian Hughes	10/1
pu		LE PREZIEN (FR)	7	11-7	(t)	Paul Nicholls	Barry Geraghty	11/1

6 ran Race Time 5m 18.60 Closing Sectional (3.15f): 49.8s (101.2%) Winning Owner: Mr J. Hales

With Altior bypassing this race in favour of the Celebration later in the month this year's Melling was dealt a small blow before the declaration stage, but it was a still a quality sextet that included Ryanair-winner Balko des Flos, Champion Chase runner-up Min and Tingle Creek-winner Politologue; the first of those disappointed but the other pair pulled well clear in what developed into a thrilling duel up the straight, and what they achieved wasn't far below the 5-year standard for the contest, which is bumped up by a huge effort from Sprinter Sacre in 2013 anyway. **Politologue** was refitted with a hood alongside a first-time tongue strap after not seeing his race out in the Champion Chase, and that combination seemed to have a positive effect as he produced his best performance yet to land a second Grade 1 of the season back up in trip, a top-class effort to beat Min and a very game one too; chased leader, travelled well, hit tenth, close up 3 out, upsides last, edged ahead run-in, proved determined; although he's a notch below the very best he is consistent and has had a tremendous season overall. **Min** is a few pounds better than Politologue at his very best but didn't quite produce that level here, his exuberance probably just telling in the finish over this trip on very testing ground; tracked pace, raced freely, close up 4 out, led going well soon after 3 out, edged out run-in, gave his all and pulled clear of the remainder; a Grade 1 win outside of novice company still eludes him but he'll take the beating back at 2m at Punchestown later this month if over these exertions. **Sizing Granite** faced a very stiff task back over fences but at least confirmed that he's back on song after winning a handicap hurdle last time; in rear, made mistakes, some headway 4 out, plugged on, made no impression; he's not one to hold his form for long, though. **Balko des Flos** showed what he's capable of in the Ryanair and that big performance must have left a mark as he simply wasn't in anything like the same form; led, headed soon after 3 out and folded. **Cloudy Dream** produced a rare below-par effort, consistency something that overall he can't be knocked for, probably over the top for the season now, but he's not the most genuine; in touch, lost place after 4 out, well held, looking half-hearted. **Le Prezien** faced a stiff task in this grade but clearly wasn't 100% on the day; held up, bad mistake ninth, pulled up quickly.

Doom Bar Sefton Novices' Hurdle (Grade 1) (1)

Pos	Btn	Horse	Age	Wgt	Eq	Trainer	Jockey	SP
1		SANTINI	6	11-4		Nicky Henderson	Nico de Boinville	6/4f
2	1½	ROKSANA (IRE)	6	10-11		Dan Skelton	Harry Skelton	9/1
3	6	TOWER BRIDGE (IRE)	5	11-4	(t)	Joseph Patrick O'Brien, Ireland	J. J. Slevin	8/1
4	2¾	UPPERTOWN PRINCE (IRE)	6	11-4		Donald McCain	Brian Hughes	40/1
5	8	OK CORRAL (IRE)	8	11-4		Nicky Henderson	Barry Geraghty	7/2
6	3¼	DANS LE VENT (FR)	5	11-4	(s)	Jamie Snowden	Gavin Sheehan	66/1
7	14	POINT OF PRINCIPLE (IRE)	5	11-4		Tim Vaughan	Alan Johns	66/1
pu		ANOTHER STOWAWAY (IRE)	6	11-4	(t)	Tom George	A. P. Heskin	50/1
pu		CHEF DES OBEAUX (FR)	6	11-4		Nicky Henderson	Noel Fehily	6/1
pu		COUNT MERIBEL	6	11-4		Nigel Twiston-Davies	Mark Grant	25/1
pu		GOOD MAN PAT (IRE)	5	11-4		Alan King	Tom Bellamy	25/1
pu		LOUSE TALK (IRE)	6	11-4		Charlie Longsdon	Paul O'Brien	66/1
pu		SAM'S GUNNER	5	11-4		Michael Easterby	William Kennedy	12/1

13 ran Race Time 6m 41.30 Closing Sectional (3.15f): 51.2s (100.0%) Winning Owner: Mr & Mrs R. Kelvin-Hughes

Plenty bombed out but at the top end this is up-to-scratch Grade 1 novice form, with the winner improving on form that saw him finish third in the Albert Barlett to get the better of a highly progressive mare who impressed greatly with how she cruised through a gruelling race run at a sound gallop. **Santini** quickly resumed progress, probably all the better for his experience in the Albert Bartlett, a more positive ride than he got in that race definitely helping as well, in that it made the most of his abundant stamina; pressed leader, taken wide and led 3 out, tackled run-in, found plenty; he'll take high rank as a staying novice chaser in 2018/19. **Roksana** had no problem with the longer trip and ran a mighty race taking on males for the first time over hurdles, really taking the eye with how she travelled, then going down fighting against a smart gelding to whom she conceded a head start; dropped out, travelled best, smooth headway home turn, closing when not clear run 2 out, challenged run-in, kept on; winning graded races against mares will be a formality for her next season. **Tower Bridge** ran every bit as well as he had at Cheltenham, again confirming that he's got plenty of stamina and needing no excuses; in touch, ridden when not fluent 3 out, blundered last, one paced; he's not as obvious a chaser as some in this field (Flat bred and lacking in size). **Uppertown Prince** showed much improved form, clearly well suited by his stiffest test of stamina so far; in touch, stumbled second, pushed along 3 out, one paced from next; he's bound to do well in novice chases next season. **Ok Corral** failed to repeat his Cheltenham effort, when he'd finished a length and a half in front of Santini, his rather tame finish suggesting he perhaps wasn't over that big performance, maybe not the biggest surprise bearing in mind he hasn't stood much racing; in touch, effort after 3 out, edged left, weakened last. **Dans Le Vent** in first-time cheekpieces, ran as well as entitled to, seemingly coming up short for ability rather than stamina; led until 3 out, weakened last. **Point of Principle** failed to repeat last effort, lack of stamina perhaps an issue, though his jumping was sloppy; pressed leader, jumped none too fluently, pushed along 3 out, weakened next. **Another Stowaway** after 10 weeks off, was out of depth; raced off the pace, struggling after 4 out. **Chef des Obeaux** bombed out for the second time in a row, leaving him with something to prove; held up, struggling after 4 out. **Count Meribel** had finished last on his last 2 outings and ran even worse after 8 weeks off, never mind that it was a stiff task; held up, ridden after 4 out, soon beaten. **Good Man Pat** found this too competitive, having done his winning in small-field novices; mid-division, not fluent ninth, struggling after 4 out. **Louse Talk** whose rider was unable to claim, hadn't done nearly enough in 2 minor wins to suggest he'd be up to this level and predictably struggled, lack of stamina not the issue; in touch, lost place from early final circuit, struggling when mistake 4 out. **Sam's Gunner** ran too badly to be true, either amiss or over the top for the season; in rear, never travelling well, beaten long way out; lack of stamina not to blame.

AINTREE Saturday April 14
SOFT

Doom Bar Maghull Novices' Chase (Grade 1) (1)

Pos	Btn	Horse	Age	Wgt	Eq	Trainer	Jockey	SP
1		DIEGO DU CHARMIL (FR)	6	11-4	(t)	Paul Nicholls	Harry Cobden	5/1
2	2½	PETIT MOUCHOIR (FR)	7	11-4		Henry de Bromhead, Ireland	Davy Russell	4/5f
3	6	SHANTOU ROCK (IRE)	6	11-4	(t)	Dan Skelton	Harry Skelton	13/2
4	nk	LADY BUTTONS	8	10-11		Philip Kirby	Adam Nicol	4/1
5	24	KAUTO RIKO (FR)	7	11-4		Tom Gretton	Robert Dunne	25/1
6	24	DELEGATE	8	11-4	(t)	Keith Dalgleish	Brian Hughes	40/1

6 ran Race Time 4m 02.40 Closing Sectional (3.15f): 47.4s (102.0%) Winning Owner: Mrs Johnny de la Hey

This looked a golden opportunity for Petit Mouchoir to gain compensation for 2 defeats at the hands of Footpad, but he got worked up beforehand and surely wasn't at his best, Diego du Charmil the one to take advantage, clearly on the upgrade himself but likely to have shown form a little below the standard for the race, this lacking depth for a Grade 1. **Diego du Charmil** had won just a match in 4 previous starts over fences, but he was obviously unfortunate last time and gained ample compensation, showing improved form up in grade, taking advantage of the favourite not being quite at his best; in touch, travelled well, not fluent 3 out, led on bridle after next, in command soon after, ridden out; he could well progress again in open company next season, the Haldon Gold Cup a likely starting point. **Petit Mouchoir** stood out on form, yet he was unable to capitalise, worked up beforehand (easy to back as a result) and failing to settle under a more restrained ride than usual, the winner clearly improved, though surely he himself again wasn't quite at his best; tracked pace, pulled hard, shaken up after 3 out, led briefly next, unable to go with winner approaching last, kept on run-in. **Shantou Rock** after 11 weeks off, ran well upped further in grade, though with no obvious excuses; led, jumped well in main (not fluent first, seventh), headed 2 out, one paced; he's won only once as a novice, in part due to being so highly tried, his jumping his main asset as he heads towards handicaps, raced only around 2m yet with elements in his pedigree suggesting he's at least worth trying over further. **Lady Buttons** had impressed in winning both her previous starts over fences, but seemed to be found out in better company this time, no obvious excuses; in touch, pushed along before 3 out, not quicken next; she obviously will have options next season, though the enhanced mares programme is largely for races over further than 2m. **Kauto Riko** had plenty to find in this higher grade and never looked likely to get involved; soon detached, tailed off before halfway. **Delegate** was out of his depth back over fences and never got involved, finishing lame; held up, bad mistake fifth, struggling when mistake seventh, tailed off after.

TIMEFORM'S BEST OF 2017/18

It was another fantastic season of National Hunt racing, one of the main highlights being Altior overcoming a delayed start to the campaign to prove himself the best 2m chaser around—and arguably the best jumper of any description—when winning the Queen Mother Champion Chase at the Cheltenham Festival. It was time to say goodbye to one of the most popular horses in recent times, too, Cue Card no longer quite the force of old although runner-up to Waiting Patiently in the Ascot Chase. He clearly wasn't himself on his final outing when pulled up in the Ryanair Chase at the Cheltenham Festival—a race he had won in 2013—and connections decided to retire him the following month after he had seemed to lose his usual spark on the gallops. Cue Card's trainer, Colin Tizzard, enjoyed another record-breaking year, though, recording 78 winners in total, surpassing his tally in the previous season by 18. The trainers' championship went right down to the wire over in Ireland, Gordon Elliott holding a healthy lead heading into the Punchestown Festival, but Willie Mullins saddled an astonishing 18 winners that week to take it away from Elliott in the dying strides; it was an eleventh trainers' title in succession for the all-conquering Mullins.

Staying chasers

For the second season running Colin Tizzard had the top staying chaser in the shape of **Native River** (c172), who was intentionally campaigned sparingly. It was a magnificent training performance from Tizzard, getting the eight-year-old to peak for the Cheltenham Gold Cup on the back of just one run, and his duel up the hill with King George winner **Might Bite** (c171) was arguably the most compelling since the days of Kauto Star and Denman, with Native River ultimately seeing it out the better to beat the strong-travelling runner-up by four and a half lengths. Might Bite went on to gain compensation with victory on his final start in the Betway Bowl at Aintree, beating **Bristol de Mai** (c165x), who was a 57-length winner of the Betfair Chase at Haydock in November, by an easy seven lengths; Nicky Henderson's charge should again be a leading player in this season's Gold Cup, especially on a sounder surface. Native River, of course, had come up short in his first Gold Cup bid, when third to **Sizing John** (c169) in 2017, and the defending champion appeared to be back as good as ever when making a winning return in the John Durkan Chase at Punchestown in December. However, he was found to be clinically abnormal post-race when below form behind **Road To Respect** (c167) in the Christmas Chase at Leopardstown later that month and was later ruled out of the Gold Cup with a pelvic injury. Road To Respect produced a career best in beating subsequent Ryanair Chase winner **Balko des Flos** (c166) at Leopardstown, continuing his remarkable rise up the chasing ranks. His fourth (on unsuitably soft ground) in the Gold Cup and third behind **Bellshill** (c168) in the Punchestown Gold Cup on his final starts suggest that he will be a force in this

Native River (right) and Might Bite jump the last as one in the Gold Cup

sphere for years to come; he is still only a seven-year-old after all. Bellshill also developed into a top-class chaser, winning two of his three starts, gaining swift compensation for his aberration in the Irish Grand National with a performance in the Punchestown Gold Cup that marks him down as a live Cheltenham Gold Cup contender in 2018/19. Others to note include **Top Notch** (c166) and **Waiting Patiently** (c168p). The former is one of the most likeable horses in training and won three times last season, including the Oaksey Chase on his final start at Sandown in April, while Waiting Patiently established himself as one of most exciting prospects around in an unbeaten campaign. Ruth Jefferson's charge passed his sternest test to date with flying colours when beating Cue Card in the Ascot Chase in February and, though ruled out of the rest of the season through injury, he remains a chaser to keep on side with the prospect of more to come.

Two-mile chasers

Altior (c179p) was named Timeform's Horse of The Year for the second season running after enjoying another unbeaten campaign, winning the Game Spirit Chase at Newbury and the Celebration Chase at Sandown—both for the second year in succession—either side of his Champion Chase victory at the Cheltenham Festival. He didn't make his reappearance until

February due to suffering a setback in the autumn (required a breathing operation) and it was a terrific training performance from Nicky Henderson to even get Altior to Cheltenham—he was also lame in his near-fore leg just two days prior to the race. In the event, Altior proved himself as good as ever to beat **Min** (c169) by seven lengths, the race living up to its top billing and then some, for all that it could have been better still had **Douvan** (165+) stayed on his feet; he was still tanking along after a 12-month absence of his own when taking a heavy fall four out. The Paul Nicholls-trained **Politologue** (c166) took advantage of the early-season absence of Altior, winning his first three starts of the campaign, notably the Tingle Creek Chase at Sandown and the Desert Orchid Chase at Kempton, both in December. However, he was simply outclassed when the two met in the Game Spirit and Champion Chase and that prompted a rethink by connections—he was promptly stepped back up in trip, winning the Melling Chase at Aintree on his final start, and is set to be tried over longer distances this season. **Un de Sceaux** (c168) is similarly versatile, but once again proved he is a top-class operator at 2m, winning a third consecutive renewal of the Clarence House Chase at Ascot in January and making all to lead home a Willie Mullins-trained one-two on his final start in the Champion Chase at Punchestown, beating Douvan by two and three quarter lengths. Mullins is also responsible for the great unknown in this division in the shape of **Great Field** (c170p), who brushed aside an 11-month absence to win his only start of the last campaign in the Webster Cup at Navan in March. He remains open to improvement and will hopefully get the chance to try his hand against the very best in 2018/19.

Footpad was unbeaten in five starts over fences this season

Novice chasers

Footpad (c174p) was undoubtedly the most impressive novice of 2017/18, taking his form to a new level when switched to fences in an unbeaten season. His standout effort came in the Arkle Chase at the Cheltenham Festival, when routing the field by 14 lengths, and he didn't need to be at his best to record his fifth win of the campaign in the Ryanair Novices' Chase at Punchestown. Such was the level of form he achieved last season, he looks sure to make his mark in top open company this term, when a clash with Altior will be one to savour. **Presenting Percy** (c164p) was another to make giant strides in his first season over fences, winning a handicap over a marathon trip at Gowran in December, but putting up his best effort in the RSA Insurance Novices' Chase at the Cheltenham Festival, when beating **Monalee** (c154p) by seven lengths. Presenting Percy is already a leading fancy for next year's Gold Cup and undoubtedly the most exciting of the up-and-comers in the staying chase division. **Terrefort** (c156p) was one of Britain's leading novices, having made the switch from France to Nicky Henderson midway through the season. His win in the Mildmay Novices' Chase at Aintree on his final start proved his stamina for 3m and it wouldn't be a surprise to see him back at Aintree over the National fences at some stage. Others to taste success at Grade 1 level in this division included, JLT Novices' Chase winner **Shattered Love** (c154), Maghull Novices' Chase hero **Diego du Charmil** (c155p) and **Sceau Royal** (c157), who won the Henry VIII Novices' Chase at Sandown in December, but missed the major spring festivals through injury. **Al Boum Photo** (c161+) and the ill-fated **Finian's Oscar** (c156) were both successful at the highest level, too, before being involved in one of the most bizarre incidents you will ever see at the Punchestown Festival, a melee that allowed **The Storyteller** (c153) through to win the Champion Novices' Chase.

Staying hurdlers

Another of the training performances of the season came from Willie Mullins, who produced **Penhill** (h164) spot on to win the Stayers' Hurdle at the Cheltenham Festival after almost a year's absence. A formerly useful handicapper on the Flat, he was, admittedly, seen to maximum effect in a race where Long Walk Hurdle winner **Sam Spinner** (h158) set only a steady pace, but there is no doubting his credentials as a two-time Cheltenham Festival winner and he went on to give another good account when chasing home stablemate **Faugheen** (h165) on his final start in the Champion Stayers' Hurdle at Punchestown. Faugheen bookended the season with two high-class performances—he won the Morgiana Hurdle, also at Punchestown, after a near two-year absence in November—and his disappointing runs at 2m in between suggest he will most likely be campaigned over staying trips for the entirety of 2018/19, though he also has the option of going novice chasing. **Apple's Jade** (h156) again proved herself one of the best of her sex in the division, winning her first three starts, before finishing a below-form third to **Benie des Dieux** (h151p) in the Mares' Hurdle at the Cheltenham Festival. The latter confirmed that form when following up in the Mares' Champion Hurdle at Punchestown in convincing fashion, clearly as good over hurdles as she is over fences, though she is reportedly set to revert to the larger obstacles this season. **L'Ami Serge** (h163) enjoyed another productive season, the highlight coming when winning the Aintree Hurdle, while **Identity Thief** (h161) appeared to relish the step up to 3m when winning the Liverpool Hurdle at the same meeting, beating the Stayers' Hurdle third **Wholestone** (h159) by five lengths; he remains unexposed as a stayer and possibly found the race coming too soon when only fourth behind Faugheen at Punchestown.

Two-mile hurdlers

It was **Buveur d'Air** (h167) who again ruled supreme in the 2m hurdle division, enjoying another unbeaten campaign. He barely came off the bridle in winning his first three starts, including the Fighting Fifth Hurdle at Newcastle and the Christmas Hurdle at Kempton, both in December, but was made to work much harder to retain his Champion Hurdle crown at the Cheltenham Festival. He and the strong-travelling **Melon** (h166) were locked in battle for almost all of the straight, but Barry Geraghty's charge stuck his neck out in gritty fashion to pull it out of the fire, with the first two pulling three lengths clear of **Mick Jazz** (h161), who had won the Ryanair Hurdle at Leopardstown in December; Buveur d'Air is as short as 5/2 in some places to emulate Istabraq and record a third Champion Hurdle win this season. One of the most heart-warming successes of the season came courtesy of Buveur d'Air's stablemate **My Tent Or Yours** (h159), who recorded his first win at

Buveur d'Air retains his Champion Hurdle crown in gritty fashion

Cheltenham from six attempts—and his first of any kind for the best part of four years—on his return in the International Hurdle in December, beating old rival **The New One** (h157) by a length and a quarter. The New One enjoyed another productive campaign of his own, with his two wins including a fourth consecutive renewal of the Champion Hurdle Trial at Haydock in February; he bypassed a fifth run in the Champion Hurdle, instead lining up in the Stayers' Hurdle at the Cheltenham Festival, but to no avail (appearing not to stay in finishing well held). **Supasundae** (h162) fared much better in the Stayers' Hurdle, beaten only two lengths in second, though connections may have been ruing not letting him take his chance in Tuesday's feature. He certainly wouldn't have been out of place, as his two starts over 2m last season resulted in wins in Ireland's two flagship races at the trip, namely the Irish Champion Hurdle at Leopardstown and the Punchestown Champion Hurdle.

Novice hurdlers

The Gordon Elliott-trained **Samcro** (h163p) was the star of this division, winning all four of his starts in novice company before falling on his final start in the aforementioned Punchestown Champion Hurdle. He had looked a really exciting prospect in his first three starts of the season in Ireland and justified his tall reputation with a dominant performance in the Ballymore Novices' Hurdle at Cheltenham, beating **Black Op** (h152) by two and three quarter lengths. Black Op confirmed the form when going on to win the Mersey Novices' Hurdle at Aintree and, having suffered no ill effects from his Punchestown mishap, Samcro remains an exciting prospect whether it be over hurdles or fences this season. **Summerville Boy** (h156p) deserved extra credit when winning the Supreme Novices' Hurdle at the Cheltenham Festival, overcoming late mistakes to reel in Betfair Hurdle winner **Kalashnikov** (h152p) in the closing stages, while **Kilbricken Storm** (h151) came out on top in the battle of the stayers in the Albert Bartlett Novices' Hurdle, though the third **Santini** (h150), who went on to win the Sefton Novices' Hurdle at Aintree, is possibly the best long-term prospect in the field. Kilbricken Strom headed to Punchestown instead of Aintree, finishing a close up third to **Next Destination** (152p) in the Irish Daily Mirror Novices' Hurdle. **Laurina** (150p) proved herself by far the best novice of her sex by winning all four of her starts by wide margins, her best effort coming in the Dawn Run Mares' Novices' Hurdle at the Cheltenham Festival, where she recorded an impressive timefigure; she'd no doubt continue to be hard to beat in mares' races, but deserves to be tested in open company at some stage. Finally, there was no standout among the juveniles, though Triumph Hurdle winner **Farclas** (153p) and **We Have A Dream** (150p), who won a pair of Grade 1s but was forced to miss Cheltenham through injury, are both open to more improvement.

GRAB THE FREE BETS

Find your winners with racing's best ratings and analysis, then 'get on' direct from the Timeform website and App.

For sign-up offers and
Timeform exclusives from our partners:

visit timeform.com/free-bets

2017/18 STATISTICS

TRAINERS (1,2,3 earnings)		Horses	Indiv'l Wnrs	Races Won	Runs	% Strike Rate	Stakes £
1	Nicky Henderson	154	85	141	524	26.9	3,376,169
2	Paul Nicholls	150	68	127	576	22.0	2,371,072
3	Colin Tizzard	111	50	79	536	14.7	1,903,524
4	Nigel Twiston-Davies	128	56	80	527	15.2	1,807,755
5	Dan Skelton	215	90	156	801	19.5	1,643,967
6	W. P. Mullins, Ireland	66	9	10	74	13.5	1,487,238
7	Gordon Elliott, Ireland	72	19	21	106	19.8	1,317,008
8	Tom George	105	34	47	356	13.2	912,070
9	Alan King	125	36	58	389	14.9	855,241
10	Donald McCain	113	58	98	539	18.2	785,839

JOCKEYS (by winners)		1st	2nd	3rd	Unpl	Total Rides	% Strike Rate
1	Richard Johnson	176	156	118	451	901	19.5
2	Brian Hughes	142	131	112	425	810	17.5
3	Harry Skelton	131	107	104	270	612	21.4
4	Noel Fehily	110	82	62	278	532	20.7
5	Sam Twiston-Davies	108	90	83	287	568	19.0
6	Aidan Coleman	104	73	84	409	670	15.5
7	Sean Bowen	82	64	55	281	482	17.0
8	Nico de Boinville	77	54	44	192	367	21.0
9	Harry Cobden	76	71	67	226	440	17.3
10	Tom Scudamore	74	82	79	375	610	12.1

SIRES OF WINNERS (1,2,3 earnings)		Races Won	Runs	% Strike Rate	Stakes £
1	King's Theatre (by Sadler's Wells)	87	697	12.5	1,675,857
2	Presenting (by Mtoto)	110	845	13.0	1,547,559
3	Kayf Tara (by Sadler's Wells)	109	885	12.3	1,436,250
4	Flemensfirth (by Alleged)	102	698	14.6	1,271,108
5	Oscar (by Sadler's Wells)	97	675	14.4	1,205,907
6	Milan (by Sadler's Wells)	107	747	14.3	1,109,135
7	Midnight Legend (by Night Shift)	101	738	13.7	1,026,603
8	Westerner (by Danehill)	98	674	14.5	1,024,539
9	Beneficial (by Top Ville)	82	645	12.7	840,544
10	Scorpion (by Montjeu)	56	428	13.1	768,609

LEADING HORSES (1,2,3 earnings)		Races Won	Runs	Stakes £
1	Tiger Roll 8 b.g Authorized–Swiss Roll	2	3	540,417
2	Buveur d'Air 7 b.g Crillon–History	4	4	413,789
3	Native River 8 ch.g Indian River–Native Mo	2	2	402,972
4	Might Bite 9 b.g Scorpion–Knotted Midge	3	4	393,103
5	Politologue 7 gr.g Poliglote–Scarlet Row	4	6	342,654
6	Altior 8 b.g High Chaparral–Monte Solaro	3	3	342,087
7	Bristol de Mai 7 gr.g Saddler Maker–La Bole Night	2	5	226,299
8	Balko des Flos 7 ch.g Balko–Royale Marie	1	2	204,015
9	Pleasant Company 10 b.g Presenting–Katie Flame	0	1	200,000
10	L'Ami Serge 8 b.g King's Theatre–La Zingarella	1	5	193,275

SECTION

5

THE TIMEFORM TOP 100

Hurdlers

Rating	Horse
167	Buveur d'Air
166	Melon
165	Faugheen
164	Penhill
163p	Samcro
163	L'Ami Serge
162	Bapaume
162	Supasundae
161	Identity Thief
161	Mick Jazz
161§	Wicklow Brave
160	Agrapart
159	My Tent Or Yours
159	Wholestone
158	Sam Spinner
157	Cilaos Emery
157	Elgin
157	The New One
156p	Summerville Boy
156	Apple's Jade
156	Beer Goggles
156	Nichols Canyon
156	The Last Samuri
155	Bacardys
154	Call Me Lord
154	Shaneshill
154	Topofthegame
154	Unowhatimeanharry
153	Coquin Mans
153	The Worlds End
153	Yanworth
152p	Kalashnikov
152	Black Op
152	Lil Rockerfeller
152	Presenting Percy
152	Swamp Fox
151p	Benie des Dieux
151p	Next Destination
151	Bleu Et Rouge
151	Campeador
151	Diamond Cauchois
151	Kilbricken Storm
151	Old Guard
150p	Cracking Smart
150p	Laurina
150p	We Have A Dream
150	Ch'tibello
150	Colin's Sister
150	Delta Work
150	John Constable
150	Santini
150	William Henry
149p	If The Cap Fits
149	Blow By Blow
149	Draconien
149	Farclas
149	Mengli Khan
149	Thomas Campbell
148	Augusta Kate
148	Cyrus Darius
148	Jezki
148	Ok Corral
148	Paloma Blue
147+	Ballyoptic
147	Bleu Berry
147	Claimantakinforgan
147	Desert Cry
147	Lalor
147	Lostintranslation
147	Mr Adjudicator
147	Remiluc
146p	Soul Emotion
146p	Vinndication
146	Dortmund Park
146	Mohaayed
146	On The Blind Side
146	Scarpeta
146	Vision des Flos
146	Who Dares Wins
145	Ballyward
145	Bunk Off Early
145	Duc des Genievres
145	La Bague Au Roi
145	Meri Devie
145	Saldier
145	Wakea
145	Western Ryder
145x	Clyne
144	Air Horse One
144	Bedrock
144	Court Minstrel
144	Donna's Diamond
144	Getabird
144	Glenloe
144	Izzo
144	Jenkins
144	Lagostovegas
144	Minella Awards
144	Pallasator
144	Rashaan
144	Taquin du Seuil
144	Tigris River

Chasers

Rating	Horse
179p	Altior
174p	Footpad
172	Native River
171	Might Bite
171	Sizing John
170p	Great Field
169	Min
169	Un de Sceaux
168p	Waiting Patiently
168	Bellshill
167	Fox Norton
167	Road To Respect
167x	Our Duke
166	Balko des Flos
166	Politologue
166	Top Notch
165+	Douvan
165	Cue Card
165	Djakadam
165	Whisper
165x	Bristol de Mai
164p	Presenting Percy
164+	Disko
164	Anibale Fly
164	Definitly Red
164§	Outlander
163+	Total Recall
163x	Killultagh Vic
162	Clan des Obeaux
162	Doctor Phoenix
162?	Double Shuffle
161+	Al Boum Photo
161	Edwulf
161	Smad Place
160	Ballyoisin
160	Blaklion
160	Coney Island
160	Frodon
160	Tea For Two
160?	Sizing Codelco
159p	Bachasson
159+	Petit Mouchoir
159	Kylemore Lough
159	Sub Lieutenant
159	The Last Samuri
159x	Minella Rocco
158+	Thistlecrack
158	San Benedeto
158	Sir Valentino
157p	Kemboy
157p	Monalee
157+	Saint Calvados
157	A Toi Phil
157	Ar Mad
157	Ball d'Arc
157	Charbel
157	Cloudy Dream
157	Sceau Royal
157	Simply Ned
157	Sizing Granite
156p	Terrefort
156	Alpha des Obeaux
156	Cyrname
156	Finian's Oscar
156	Starchitect
156x	Le Prezien
155p	Diego du Charmil
155	Art Mauresque
155	Gold Present
155	Mala Beach
155	Ordinary World
155	Sandymount Duke
155	Shantou Flyer
155	Special Tiara
155	Tiger Roll
154+	Death Duty
154+	God's Own

154	Ballyoptic
154	Brain Power
154	Devils Bride
154	Forest Bihan
154	Hammersly Lake
154	Invitation Only
154	Shattered Love
154	Valseur Lido
153+	American
153+	L'Ami Serge
153	Ballycasey
153	Dounikos
153	Fountains Windfall
153	Gino Trail
153	Perfect Candidate
153	Rathvinden
153	Speredek
153	The Storyteller
152p	Rather Be
152	Flying Angel
152	Pleasant Company
152	Shaneshill
152	Top Gamble
152§	Regal Encore

Juvenile Hurdlers

150p	We Have A Dream
149	Farclas
147	Mr Adjudicator
145	Saldier
142	Espoir d'Allen
142	Sayo
141	Redicean
140	Gumball
138	Mitchouka
138	Saglawy
137	Apple's Shakira
137	Stormy Ireland
136	Beau Gosse
136	Msassa
134	Style de Garde
133	Malaya
132	Act of Valour
131	Nube Negra
131	Sussex Ranger
130	Veneer of Charm
129	Casa Tall
128p	Albert's Back
127p	The Statesman

127	City Dreamer
127	Crucial Moment
127	Doctor Bartolo
127	Look My Way
127	Taxmeifyoucan

Novice Hurdlers

163p	Samcro
156p	Summerville Boy
152p	Kalashnikov
152	Black Op
151p	Next Destination
151	Kilbricken Storm
150p	Cracking Smart
150p	Laurina
150	Delta Work
150	Santini
149p	If The Cap Fits
149	Blow By Blow
149	Draconien
149	Mengli Khan
148	Ok Corral
148	Paloma Blue
147	Claimantakinforgan
147	Lalor
147	Lostintranslation
146p	Vinndication
146	Dortmund Park
146	On The Blind Side
146	Scarpeta
146	Vision des Flos
145	Ballyward
145	Duc des Genievres
145	Western Ryder
144	Bedrock
144	Getabird
144	Pallasator

Novice Chasers

174p	Footpad
164p	Presenting Percy
161+	Al Boum Photo
159+	Petit Mouchoir
157p	Kemboy
157p	Monalee
157+	Saint Calvados
157	Sceau Royal
156p	Terrefort

156	Cyrname
156	Finian's Oscar
155p	Diego du Charmil
154+	Death Duty
154	Ballyoptic
154	Brain Power
154	Invitation Only
154	Shattered Love
153	Dounikos
153	Fountains Windfall
153	Rathvinden
153	The Storyteller
152p	Rather Be
151+	Bamako Moriviere
151	Black Corton
151	Elegant Escape
150p	Benatar
150+	Jury Duty
150+	Ozzie The Oscar
150+	Yanworth
150	Dolos

NH Flat Horses

125	Tornado Flyer
123	Blackbow
123	Carefully Selected
119	Rhinestone
118	Acey Milan
116	Relegate
115	Getaway John
115	Hollowgraphic
114	Downtown Getaway
113	Brace Yourself
113	Good Boy Bobby
113	Rapid Escape
112p	Brewin'upastorm
112	Caribert
112	Felix Desjy
112	Minella Encore
112	Portrush Ted
111+	Didtheyleaveuoutto
110	Voix des Tiep
109	Mercy Mercy Me
108	Bullionaire
108	Getaway Katie Mai
108	Harambe
108	Kalum River
108	Kateson
108	Two For Gold

107p	Commander of Fleet
107p	Dream Conti
107p	Seddon
107p	Time To Move On
107	Black Pirate
107	Clinton Hill
107	Colreevy
107	Crooks Peak
107	Gallahers Cross
107	Posh Trish
107	Queenohearts
107	Queens Cave
107	The Big Bite
107	The Flying Sofa

Hunter Chasers

134+	Gilgamboa
134	Pacha du Polder
133	Creevytennant
133	Grand Vision
133	Midnight Cowboy
132p	Burning Ambition
131	Marinero
130	Galway Jack
130	Unioniste
129	Barel of Laughs
129	Cousin Pete
129	Kilfinichen Bay
129	Mendip Express
129	O Maonlai
129	Shotavodka
129	Wells de Lune
128	Balnaslow
128	Sir Jack Yeats
127	Full Trottle
126	Barrakilla
126	Bear's Affair
126	Darwins Fox
126	Double Whammy
126	Foxrock
126	Kilbree Kid
126	Virak
126	Young Hurricane
125p	Duhallow Tornado
125	Rebel Rebellion
124	Cultram Abbey

* Indicates best performance achieved in a race other than a hunter chase

PROMISING HORSES

A p symbol is used by Timeform to denote horses we believe are capable of improvement, with a P symbol suggesting a horse is capable of much better form. Below is a list of selected British and Irish-trained horses with a p or P, listed under their current trainers.

KIM BAILEY

Cloone Lady (IRE) 6 b.m. h113p
Diva Reconce (FR) 5 b.m. h105p
Red River (IRE) 5 ch.g. h139p
Vinndication (IRE) 5 b.g. h146p b96
Wandrin Star (IRE) 7 b.g. h80p c113

GILLIAN BOANAS

Crixus's Escape (IRE) 5 ch.g. h121p
Just Call Me Al (IRE) 5 br.g. b90p
Penny Blak 5 ch.g. b89p

MARK BRADSTOCK

Step Back (IRE) 8 ch.g. c146p

DAVID BRIDGWATER

Cohesion 5 b.g. h99p
Dame du Soir (FR) 5 br.m. h98p
The Tin Miner (IRE) 7 br.g. c109p

HENRY DE BROMHEAD, IRELAND

Monalee (IRE) 7 b.g. c157p
Twobeelucky 5 b.g. h134p

MICK CHANNON

Mister Whitaker (IRE) 6 b.g. c146p

REBECCA CURTIS

Geordie des Champs (IRE) 7 br.g. ... c135p
Sunset Showdown (IRE) 5 b.g. .. h119p b93

KEITH DALGLEISH

One Night In Milan (IRE) 5 b.g. h82p b76
Senor Lombardy (IRE) 5 b.g. h131p b103
The Vocalist 6 b.m. h115p

HENRY DALY

Back To The Thatch (IRE) 6 b.g. c127p
Honest Vic (IRE) 5 b.g. h122p b90

GORDON ELLIOTT, IRELAND

Commander of Fleet (IRE) 4 b.g. .. b107p
Cracking Smart (FR) 6 b. or br.g. .. h150p
Flawless Escape 5 gr.g. h131p b99
Master of Tara (FR) 5 b.g. b106p
Minellafordollars (IRE) 6 b.g. h129p
Monbeg Worldwide (IRE) 6 b.g. ... h130p
Samcro (IRE) 6 ch.g. h163p
Sutton Place (IRE) 7 b.g. c145p
Veinard (FR) 9 ch.g. h125 c127p

BRIAN ELLISON

Bowban 4 b.c. h58p
Snookered (IRE) 4 b.g. h62p
Tomngerry (IRE) 8 b.g. h132 c108p
Windsor Avenue (IRE) 6 b.g. b104p

P. A. FAHY, IRELAND

Castlegrace Paddy (IRE) 7 b.g. c145p
Dunvegan (FR) 5 gr.g. h122p b112

HARRY FRY

Acting Lass (IRE) 7 b.g. c149p
Chalonnial (FR) 6 ch.g. c124P
If The Cap Fits (IRE) 6 b.g. h149p
Samarquand 4 b. or br.g. b103p

TOM GEORGE

Boyhood (IRE) 7 b.g. h135p
Cuirassier Dempire (FR) 6 ch.g. ... c134p
Drill Baby Drill 7 b.m. h92p
Espoir de Teillee (FR) 6 b.g. h124p
Forgot To Ask (IRE) 6 b.g. h109p
Mzuzu (IRE) 6 b.g. h117p b66p
Seddon (FR) 5 b.g. b107p
Strike In Milan (IRE) 6 b.g. b84p
Summerville Boy (IRE) 6 b.g. h156p b98

WARREN GREATREX

Another Emotion (FR) 6 gr.g. h113p
Don des Fosses (FR) 5 b.g. ... h71p b94
The Butcher Said (IRE) 5 b.g. . h80p b91

ALEX HALES

Quarry Leader (IRE) 7 b.g. h112p
Royal Sunday (FR) 4 gr.g. h108p
Shazzamataz (FR) 6 br.m h104p

NICKY HENDERSON

Casablanca Mix (FR) 6 ch.m. c141p
Champ (IRE) 6 b.g. h134p
Dame de Compagnie (FR) 5 b.m. .. h131p
Diese des Bieffes (FR) 5 gr.g. h136p
Divine Spear (IRE) 7 b.g. c143p
Du Destin (FR) 5 gr.g. h73p
Fixe Le Kap (FR) 6 gr.g. h138 c126p
French Crusader (FR) 5 b.g. . h122p b95
Lust For Glory (IRE) 5 b.m. b86p
Rather Be (IRE) 7 b.g. c152p
River Wylde (IRE) 7 b.g. c140p
Settle Hill (USA) 5 b.g. h128p
Soul Emotion (FR) 5 b.g. h146p
Tell It To Me 6 b.m. h73p b98
Terrefort (FR) 5 gr.g. h124 c156p
The Bottom Bar (IRE) 6 br.g. . h122p b91
Turn Turk (IRE) 7 gr.m. h116p
Turtle Wars (FR) 5 b.g. h116p
We Have A Dream (FR) 4 b.g. h150p
Whatswrongwithyou (IRE) 7 ch.g. h128p
With Discretion (IRE) 7 b.m. h128p

PHILIP HOBBS

Dostal Phil (FR) 5 b.g. h107p
Festival Dawn 6 b.m. h112p

For Good Measure (IRE) 7 b.g. c132p
Gosheven (IRE) 5 b.g. h125p b72
Horse Force One (IRE) 7 b.g. . h91p b96
Little Rory Mac (IRE) 4 b.g. b91p
Longtown (IRE) 7 b.g. c122p
Lord Duveen (IRE) 5 br.g. h116p
No Comment 7 b.m. c122P
Scoop The Pot (IRE) 8 b.g. .. h126 c121p
Steely Addition (IRE) 6 b.g. h128p
Strong Pursuit (IRE) 8 ch.g. c139p
Turangi 6 b.g. h109p
Umndeni (FR) 4 b. or br.g. b101p

ANTHONY HONEYBALL

My Dance 6 b.m. h114p b78
Represented (IRE) 5 b.g. b92p
Sam Brown 6 b.g. h135p

RUTH JEFFERSON

Temple Man 6 b.g. h95p
Waiting Patiently (IRE) 7 b.g. c168p

PATRICK G. KELLY, IRELAND

Presenting Percy 7 b.g. h152 c164p

ALAN KING

Ballywood (FR) 4 b.g. h121 c117p
Cosmeapolitan 5 b.g. h119p
Deyrann de Carjac (FR) 5 b.g. h119p b97
Dingo Dollar (IRE) 6 ch.g. c147p
Dusky Legend 8 b.m. h123 c143p
Full Glass (FR) 5 b.g. h124 c141p
Kozier (GER) 4 ch.g. h111p
Nobby 4 b.g. b89p
Paddy Boss (IRE) 6 ch.g. b99p
Potterman 5 b.g. h113p b101
Stylish Moment (IRE) 5 b.g. . h106p b96
Tillythetank (IRE) 5 b.m. h80p
Yesandno (IRE) 5 b.g. b65p

TOM LACEY

Mary Eleanor 6 b.m. h101p b86
Sebastopol (IRE) 4 b.g. b101p
Thomas Patrick (IRE) 6 b.g. . h123 c147p
Triopas (IRE) 6 b.g. h104 c110p

EMMA LAVELLE

Gunfleet (IRE) 6 b.g. h130p
Majestic Moll (IRE) 6 b.m. h112p

CHARLIE LONGSDON

Ballydine (IRE) 8 ch.g. c133p
Braddan Head 5 br.g. h97p
Djarkevi (FR) 5 b.g. h98p
Midnight Sonata (IRE) 4 b.g. b90p
Stormy Milan (IRE) 5 b.g. h102p b69

DONALD McCAIN

Gray Day (IRE) 7 gr.g. c122p
Mount Mews (IRE) 7 b.g. h138 c138p
O'Hanrahan Bridge (IRE) 6 b.g. b94p
Spin The Coin (IRE) 5 b.g. h105p
Swashbuckle 5 b.g. h106p
The Great Getaway (IRE) 6 b.g. h114p b76

NOEL MEADE, IRELAND

De Name Escapes Me (IRE) 8 ch.g. h133 c112p
Dream Conti (FR) 5 br.g. b107p

GARY MOORE

Age of Wisdom (IRE) 5 ch.g. h66p
Altaayil (IRE) 7 br.g. h83p
Benatar (IRE) 6 b.g. c150p
Bridle Loanan (IRE) 5 b.g. b77p
Iballisticvin 5 b.g. h91p
Not Another Muddle 7 b.g. c131p

M. F. MORRIS, IRELAND

Grotesque 7 b.g. h114p

NEIL MULHOLLAND

Better News 7 b.m. h81p
Inaminna (IRE) 7 b.g. h116p b68
Kalondra (IRE) 7 b.g. c147p
Meribel Millie 7 b.m. c83p
Milkwood (IRE) 4 b.g. b86p
Mind Your Back (IRE) 5 b.g. b84p
Neachells Bridge (IRE) 6 ch.g. h108p b97
Niblawi (IRE) 6 b.g. h123p

W. P. MULLINS, IRELAND

Bacardys (FR) 7 b. or br.g. .. h155 c136p
Bachasson (FR) 7 gr.g. c159p
Benie des Dieux (FR) 7 b.m h151p c148P
Blazer (FR) 7 ch.g. c137p
Brahma Bull (IRE) 7 ch.g. h126p b111
Bunk Off Early (IRE) 6 ro.g. .. h145 c138p
Cadmium (FR) 6 b.g. c148p
Childrens List (IRE) 8 b.g. c146p
Deal d'Estruval (FR) 5 b.g. h134p
Footpad (FR) 6 b.g. c174p
Great Field (FR) 7 b.g. c170p
Kemboy (FR) 6 b.g. c157p
Laurina (FR) 5 b.m. h150p
Mystic Theatre (IRE) 7 b.m.. h135p b103
Next Destination (IRE) 6 b.g. h151p
Patricks Park (IRE) 7 b.g. h90 c141p
Pleasure Dome 5 b.m. h105p
Stratum 5 b.g. h131p
Tin Soldier (FR) 7 b.g. c135p
Total Recall (IRE) 9 b.g. ...... h143p c163+
Turcagua (FR) 8 gr.g. c133p

AMY MURPHY

Kalashnikov (IRE) 5 br.g. h152p

OLLY MURPHY

Ballinslea Bridge (IRE) 6 b.g. h125p b94p
Brewin'upastorm (IRE) 5 b.g. b112p
General Bux 7 b.g. h94p
Sangha River (IRE) 5 br.g. b103p
The Very Thing (IRE) 4 b.g. b84p
Weebill 6 b.g. h116p b96

DR RICHARD NEWLAND

Capitoul (FR) 6 b.g. h109 c126p
Competition 6 b.g. h103p
Slim Pickens (IRE) 10 b.g. h130 c118p

PAUL NICHOLLS

Bill And Barn (IRE) 7 br.g. h111 c121p
Brio Conti (FR) 7 gr.g. c129P
Chameron (FR) 5 b.g. c132p
Danny Kirwan (IRE) 5 b.g. b103P
Diamond Guy (FR) 5 b.g. h115p
Diego du Charmil (FR) 6 b.g. c155p
El Bandit (IRE) 7 b. or br.g. c141p
Emerging Talent (IRE) 9 b.g. c126p
Give Me A Copper (IRE) 8 ch.g. c140p
Jessber's Dream (IRE) 8 b.m. h135 c125p
Kapcorse (FR) 5 br.g. h103 c125p
Magoo (IRE) 6 gr.g. h121p
Master Tommytucker 7 b.g. h129p
Rock On Oscar (IRE) 8 b.g. c116p
Some Man (IRE) 5 b.g. h109p
The Last But One (IRE) 6 b.g. . h96 c132p
Truckers Lodge (IRE) 6 b.g. h111p
Worthy Farm (IRE) 5 b.g. h113p

FERGAL O'BRIEN

De Name Evades Me (IRE) 6 b.g. h115p
Jarveys Plate (IRE) 5 ch.g. b104p
Sissinghurst (IRE) 8 b.g. h105p
Time To Move On (IRE) 5 ch.g. b107p

JOSEPH PATRICK O'BRIEN, IRELAND

Lone Wolf (IRE) 5 b.g. h126p b106
Los Alamos (IRE) 5 b.g. h103p b111
Shady Operator (IRE) 5 b.g. h135p
Speak Easy 5 b.g. h141p

JONJO O'NEILL

Call To Order 8 b.g. h118 c117p
Fleminport (IRE) 8 b.g. h124p
For Instance (IRE) 8 b.g. h119 c125p
Minotaur (IRE) 6 b.g. h121p
Santiago de Cuba (IRE) 5 b.g. h99p b110
Scottshill (IRE) 6 ch.g. h83p b92

BEN PAULING

Brave Dancing 4 b.g. h115 c101p
My Turgeon (FR) 5 gr.g. b66p
Whin Park 6 b.g. h102 c79p
Willoughby Court (IRE) 7 b.g. c149p

DAVID PIPE

Buster Edwards (IRE) 5 b.g. h104p
Crawfords Mill (IRE) 6 br.m. .. h96 c96p
Mr Big Shot (IRE) 7 br.g. h142p
Rod's Dream 5 ch.g. b66p
Take The High Road 4 b.g. h85p
Whitley Neill (IRE) 6 b.g. h112p

LUCINDA RUSSELL

Grand Morning 6 b.g. h123p
Thepensionfund (IRE) 6 b.g. b91p

OLIVER SHERWOOD

Dominateur (FR) 5 b.g. b93p
Toviere (IRE) 7 ch.g. h118 c130p

DAN SKELTON

Aintree My Dream (FR) 8 b. or br.g. c132p
Anytime Will Do (IRE) 5 b.g. b103p
Beakstown (IRE) 5 b.g. b95p
Cosy Club (IRE) 4 br.g. h101p
Elton des Mottes (FR) 4 b.g. b91p
Etamine du Cochet (FR) 4 gr.f. h103p
Ferrobin (IRE) 4 br.g. b87p
Finley's Eyes (IRE) 5 b.g. b87p
Floki 4 b.g. b86p
Idee de Garde (FR) 5 b.g. b93p
Kereman (IRE) 4 b.g. h94p
Must Havea Flutter (IRE) 6 b.g. h93 c124p
New Quay (IRE) 5 b.g. h112p
Not That Fuisse (FR) 5 b.g. h107p
Present Ranger (IRE) 5 b.g. h114p
Rebel Royal (IRE) 5 b.g. h115p b76
Renwick (IRE) 5 b.g. b80p
Robin Waters (FR) 5 b.g. h140p
Stowaway Magic (IRE) 7 b.g. h135 c132p
Zamparelli (IRE) 6 b.g. h76 c111p

JAMIE SNOWDEN

Alrightjack 4 b.g. b95p
Kalahari Queen 5 br.m. h125p

COLIN TIZZARD

Ainchea (IRE) 5 b.g. h136p b104
Kings Walk (IRE) 7 b.g. h120 c106p
The Russian Doyen (IRE) 5 b.g. h123p b96
White Moon (GER) 6 gr.g. h127p

NIGEL TWISTON-DAVIES

Ballymoy (IRE) 5 b.g. h136p b92p
Chase Me (IRE) 7 b.g. h81 c74p
Imperial Acolyte 4 b.g. b64p
Imperial Nemesis (IRE) 5 b.g h104p b86
Luckofthedraw (FR) 5 gr.g. ... h118p b95
One For Rosie 5 gr.g. b100p

HARRY WHITTINGTON

Carole's Vigilante (IRE) 7 ch.g. h110p
Court Liability (IRE) 5 b.g. . h120p b102
Djin Conti (FR) 5 b.g. h99p
Jumbo Davis (IRE) 5 b.m. b63p

EVAN WILLIAMS

Billy Bronco 7 b.g. c116p
Bold Plan (IRE) 4 b.g. b103p
Clyne 8 b.g. h145x c134p
Court Royale (IRE) 5 b.g. b95p

IAN WILLIAMS

Almost Gold (IRE) 5 b.g. h87p
Cause Toujours (FR) 6 b.g. h114p
Don't Act Up 7 gr.g. h89p
King of Realms (IRE) 6 b.g. h126p
The Statesman 4 b.g. h127p
Tikk Tock Boom (IRE) 6 gr.m. h96p

NOEL WILLIAMS

Breaking Waves (IRE) 4 b.g. b102p
Briery Express 5 b.m. b86p
Briery Queen 9 b.m. c140p
Drunken Pirate 5 b.g. b94p

VENETIA WILLIAMS

Belami des Pictons (FR) 7 b.g. c150p
Dark Force (FR) 5 gr.g. h76p
Shalakar (FR) 5 b.g. h121p

How's Fehily from the front?

READ THE RIDER'S RADAR

Check out the Jockey & Trainer Dashboard

Only at timeform.com

PLAY SMARTER

TRAINERS FOR COURSES

The following statistics show the most successful trainers over the past five seasons at each of the courses that stage National Hunt racing in England, Scotland and Wales. Impact Value is expressed as a factor of a trainer's number of winners compared to those expected to occur by chance. Market Value is expressed as the factor by which the % chance of an Industry Starting Price exceeds random, as implied by field size. For example, a horse that is shorter than 3/1 in a 4-runner field will have a Market Value above 1.

AINTREE

Trainer	Wins	Runs	Strike Rate	% Rivals Beaten	P/L	Run To Form %	Impact Value	Market Value
Nicky Henderson	30	151	19.87%	57.45	15.23	24.91	2.09	1.78
Paul Nicholls	18	161	11.18%	54.08	-50.38	15.68	1.21	1.66
Tom George	13	73	17.81%	57.90	35.24	28.05	2.03	1.49
Jonjo O'Neill	12	97	12.37%	47.66	-32.78	19.09	1.29	1.45
Colin Tizzard	12	56	21.43%	60.56	92.49	30.36	2.56	1.32
Philip Hobbs	11	101	10.89%	51.39	-23.05	16.07	1.33	1.45
Nigel Twiston-Davies	11	104	10.58%	57.05	-35.81	20.98	1.17	1.52
W. P. Mullins, Ireland	10	62	16.13%	59.20	-14.15	30.65	1.98	2.08
Dan Skelton	9	79	11.39%	57.76	-40.83	23.21	1.09	1.46
Peter Bowen	8	75	10.67%	51.83	-34.75	20.41	1.09	1.27

ASCOT

Trainer	Wins	Runs	Strike Rate	% Rivals Beaten	P/L	Run To Form %	Impact Value	Market Value
Nicky Henderson	31	162	19.14%	59.82	-43.15	30.62	1.58	1.85
Paul Nicholls	31	158	19.62%	58.09	-22.05	33.97	1.42	1.50
Harry Fry	15	56	26.79%	64.52	7.54	39.99	2.34	1.84
Philip Hobbs	14	94	14.89%	61.27	-8.39	27.02	1.22	1.39
Venetia Williams	14	81	17.28%	53.97	43.50	29.63	1.52	1.20
Alan King	11	80	13.75%	57.69	-26.13	26.41	1.21	1.59
David Pipe	10	64	15.63%	54.73	-4.03	19.87	1.51	1.22
Colin Tizzard	8	67	11.94%	51.65	-7.72	35.03	0.93	1.01
Gary Moore	8	87	9.20%	41.37	-31.25	17.70	0.76	0.81
Charlie Longsdon	7	62	11.29%	44.16	14.50	19.76	0.98	1.08

AYR

Trainer	Wins	Runs	Strike Rate	% Rivals Beaten	P/L	Run To Form %	Impact Value	Market Value
Nicky Richards	39	158	24.68%	57.81	-12.53	37.58	1.83	1.93
Lucinda Russell	35	294	11.90%	52.29	-130.46	25.58	0.85	1.12
N. W. Alexander	24	214	11.21%	48.13	-57.73	21.38	0.85	0.95
Stuart Crawford, Ireland	18	132	13.64%	55.30	-48.88	31.09	1.03	1.28
Donald McCain	18	93	19.35%	49.11	-31.82	26.68	1.35	1.49
James Ewart	13	100	13.00%	55.09	-16.20	23.61	1.04	1.10
Paul Nicholls	12	49	24.49%	55.33	28.88	28.57	2.37	1.63
Jim Goldie	12	107	11.21%	48.33	-44.08	21.88	0.89	1.13
Iain Jardine	10	53	18.87%	54.36	2.23	29.39	1.54	1.17
Dan Skelton	10	46	21.74%	62.05	-6.01	36.96	1.77	1.77

BANGOR-ON-DEE

Trainer	Wins	Runs	Strike Rate	% Rivals Beaten	P/L	Run To Form %	Impact Value	Market Value
Donald McCain	65	321	20.25%	56.11	28.79	29.85	1.33	1.33
Dan Skelton	21	76	27.63%	65.57	1.87	43.80	2.14	1.90
Rebecca Curtis	18	77	23.38%	58.65	-8.28	35.15	1.54	1.60
Alan King	17	60	28.33%	67.97	19.19	41.79	2.06	1.94
Jonjo O'Neill	16	119	13.45%	50.08	-27.50	20.86	1.03	1.30
Warren Greatrex	13	46	28.26%	61.17	13.39	31.78	2.08	2.01
Charlie Longsdon	13	65	20.00%	53.51	-18.61	28.28	1.32	1.43
Nigel Twiston-Davies	13	65	20.00%	63.77	5.64	35.77	1.54	1.61
Venetia Williams	11	99	11.11%	51.15	-39.01	22.69	0.82	1.11
Henry Daly	11	55	20.00%	55.04	27.00	35.70	1.55	1.24

CARLISLE

Trainer	Wins	Runs	Strike Rate	% Rivals Beaten	P/L	Run To Form %	Impact Value	Market Value
Donald McCain	35	211	16.59%	57.55	-33.63	25.95	1.16	1.44
Nicky Richards	20	90	22.22%	56.35	14.52	31.42	1.66	1.47
Sue Smith	18	121	14.88%	51.62	-28.59	24.50	1.13	1.24
Stuart Crawford, Ireland	12	31	38.71%	69.42	10.14	47.38	2.78	2.09
Brian Ellison	11	64	17.19%	56.51	-25.79	29.82	1.37	1.67
Lucinda Russell	11	167	6.59%	48.03	-98.30	20.36	0.54	1.08
Jennie Candlish	10	73	13.70%	54.62	-26.13	19.06	1.12	1.04
Micky Hammond	10	108	9.26%	42.26	-53.02	16.03	0.66	0.86
Rose Dobbin	10	77	12.99%	53.17	-24.75	21.85	1.11	1.22
Charlie Longsdon	9	30	30.00%	68.79	-13.32	39.70	2.16	2.75

CARTMEL

Trainer	Wins	Runs	Strike Rate	% Rivals Beaten	P/L	Run To Form %	Impact Value	Market Value
Donald McCain	22	122	18.03%	58.06	-25.25	20.87	1.28	1.50
James Moffatt	22	164	13.41%	52.79	0.13	20.64	1.05	1.09
Peter Bowen	13	45	28.89%	65.89	12.88	35.56	2.37	1.95
Gordon Elliott, Ireland	10	39	25.64%	70.37	-5.55	45.99	2.09	2.42
Dianne Sayer	10	104	9.62%	47.61	-46.67	17.48	0.80	1.10
Martin Todhunter	9	52	17.31%	58.63	-6.13	27.44	1.43	1.32
Kenneth Slack	8	23	34.78%	59.47	51.00	39.13	3.25	1.56
Jonjo O'Neill	7	26	26.92%	63.92	2.80	30.77	1.91	1.84
Micky Hammond	6	55	10.91%	43.83	-13.25	16.67	0.92	1.05
Brian Ellison	5	31	16.13%	57.75	-10.00	22.58	1.21	1.80

CATTERICK BRIDGE

Trainer	Wins	Runs	Strike Rate	% Rivals Beaten	P/L	Run To Form %	Impact Value	Market Value
Donald McCain	39	175	22.29%	59.91	-10.49	35.16	1.62	1.48
Sue Smith	30	101	29.70%	65.41	78.71	41.09	2.27	1.46
Brian Ellison	19	69	27.54%	66.08	-13.57	42.47	2.02	2.05
Micky Hammond	13	157	8.28%	46.81	-51.00	17.45	0.70	0.77
Dan Skelton	8	29	27.59%	61.51	-7.61	31.03	1.93	2.59
Kenneth Slack	8	33	24.24%	66.98	7.25	42.42	2.01	1.77
Jonjo O'Neill	7	34	20.59%	58.67	-4.84	42.10	1.35	1.46
Pam Sly	5	13	38.46%	70.58	11.56	61.54	3.03	1.91
Alan King	4	6	66.67%	88.61	1.74	83.33	4.87	3.84
Dianne Sayer	4	35	11.43%	51.27	56.00	20.00	1.02	0.98

CHELTENHAM

Trainer	Wins	Runs	Strike Rate	% Rivals Beaten	P/L	Run To Form %	Impact Value	Market Value
Paul Nicholls	44	391	11.25%	54.74	-1.62	25.71	1.14	1.47
Nicky Henderson	43	380	11.32%	55.44	-158.18	24.67	1.31	1.65
Philip Hobbs	34	260	13.08%	56.90	-35.25	24.88	1.52	1.51
W. P. Mullins, Ireland	34	283	12.01%	56.73	-55.61	31.80	1.70	1.93
Nigel Twiston-Davies	28	267	10.49%	49.98	-91.62	22.96	1.08	1.27
David Pipe	23	218	10.55%	50.36	-10.47	19.28	1.30	1.46
Colin Tizzard.	21	216	9.72%	50.39	-69.85	22.98	1.02	1.10
Gordon Elliott, Ireland	21	142	14.79%	60.48	72.85	30.99	2.15	1.87
Jonjo O'Neill	21	200	10.50%	48.61	-18.79	19.00	1.36	1.30
Alan King	19	179	10.61%	53.39	-37.17	25.22	1.25	1.23

CHEPSTOW

Trainer	Wins	Runs	Strike Rate	% Rivals Beaten	P/L	Run To Form %	Impact Value	Market Value
Evan Williams	32	192	16.67%	55.31	38.49	25.72	1.44	1.34
Philip Hobbs	31	152	20.39%	60.43	-30.74	33.02	1.92	2.08
Paul Nicholls	27	143	18.88%	57.90	-39.96	28.28	1.68	2.13
Peter Bowen	21	116	18.10%	56.26	21.53	30.43	1.71	1.24
Venetia Williams	18	121	14.88%	53.29	-24.98	25.86	1.30	1.27
Nigel Twiston-Davies	18	114	15.79%	59.38	-5.11	24.81	1.54	1.44
David Pipe	17	109	15.60%	62.05	-14.17	25.54	1.52	1.64
Rebecca Curtis	15	128	11.72%	57.77	-48.27	24.84	1.04	1.82
Jonjo O'Neill	15	120	12.50%	53.14	-40.71	22.06	1.26	1.44
Colin Tizzard	15	164	9.15%	55.60	-80.00	25.62	0.85	1.34

DONCASTER

Trainer	Wins	Runs	Strike Rate	% Rivals Beaten	P/L	Run To Form %	Impact Value	Market Value
Nicky Henderson	36	102	35.29%	70.48	34.35	57.90	2.76	2.73
Alan King	25	106	23.58%	62.91	28.72	33.80	1.94	1.71
Paul Nicholls	15	78	19.23%	51.27	-27.08	29.02	1.26	1.81
Emma Lavelle	14	49	28.57%	62.38	11.58	36.73	2.88	1.88
Jonjo O'Neill	12	106	11.32%	52.89	-32.84	19.28	1.14	1.09
Ben Pauling	10	46	21.74%	48.57	3.15	30.35	2.00	1.47
Kim Bailey	10	59	16.95%	55.64	2.10	32.96	1.50	1.61
Ian Williams	10	76	13.16%	47.52	-1.88	22.00	1.16	0.91
Harry Fry	9	25	36.00%	62.01	4.92	48.00	2.45	1.99
Nicky Richards	9	46	19.57%	54.04	13.25	32.56	1.99	1.23

EXETER

Trainer	Wins	Runs	Strike Rate	% Rivals Beaten	P/L	Run To Form %	Impact Value	Market Value
Philip Hobbs	44	220	20.00%	60.45	-44.12	35.74	1.66	1.97
Paul Nicholls	40	141	28.37%	64.15	-30.23	41.90	1.91	2.65
Harry Fry	27	71	38.03%	74.37	49.78	58.04	3.35	2.77
David Pipe	26	207	12.56%	52.07	-49.12	22.15	1.14	1.44
Colin Tizzard	24	172	13.95%	58.74	-77.61	24.31	1.15	1.47
Alan King	17	91	18.68%	61.96	-21.57	38.67	1.60	1.85
Susan Gardner	15	124	12.10%	47.93	-34.04	19.05	1.13	0.90
Venetia Williams	15	89	16.85%	54.38	9.96	28.30	1.41	1.29
Evan Williams	15	64	23.44%	52.95	24.38	30.53	1.74	1.26
Victor Dartnall	12	104	11.54%	53.86	-50.63	27.44	1.07	1.26

TRAINERS FOR COURSES

FAKENHAM

Trainer	Wins	Runs	Strike Rate	% Rivals Beaten	P/L	Run To Form %	Impact Value	Market Value
Lucy Wadham	20	73	27.40%	61.65	20.35	38.62	1.89	1.50
Dan Skelton	17	62	27.42%	64.14	-2.92	35.48	1.60	1.80
Neil Mulholland	15	49	30.61%	58.96	9.26	38.78	1.99	1.55
Olly Murphy	15	48	31.25%	64.75	19.94	42.50	1.77	1.40
Nicky Henderson	13	36	36.11%	68.30	-10.05	40.28	2.15	2.61
Neil King	13	85	15.29%	51.90	24.23	21.86	0.97	1.01
David Pipe	8	16	50.00%	78.02	1.22	57.81	2.46	2.17
Tim Vaughan	7	53	13.21%	47.71	-31.65	17.45	0.85	1.37
Paul Nicholls	7	20	35.00%	59.81	-0.70	45.00	1.58	1.81
Alex Hales	6	41	14.63%	55.40	-5.27	24.39	1.04	1.13

FFOS LAS

Trainer	Wins	Runs	Strike Rate	% Rivals Beaten	P/L	Run To Form %	Impact Value	Market Value
Peter Bowen	50	275	18.18%	59.03	-19.48	31.84	1.31	1.26
Evan Williams	41	319	12.85%	50.58	-82.33	21.30	0.93	1.20
Nigel Twiston-Davies	36	174	20.69%	58.25	9.84	32.01	1.48	1.39
Rebecca Curtis	34	143	23.78%	60.98	9.68	33.78	1.78	1.76
Jonjo O'Neill	18	108	16.67%	55.26	-30.97	26.09	1.27	1.52
Debra Hamer	14	82	17.07%	45.61	17.13	28.11	1.33	0.93
Bernard Llewellyn	13	93	13.98%	52.45	5.02	23.42	0.94	0.91
Tim Vaughan	12	157	7.64%	44.26	-88.02	16.76	0.56	1.07
David Pipe	12	95	12.63%	53.93	-34.16	23.41	1.00	1.61
Nicky Henderson	11	30	36.67%	65.39	-7.39	57.37	2.70	2.97

FONTWELL PARK

Trainer	Wins	Runs	Strike Rate	% Rivals Beaten	P/L	Run To Form %	Impact Value	Market Value
Gary Moore	50	345	14.49%	52.27	-60.22	25.51	1.08	1.31
Chris Gordon	41	284	14.44%	51.62	-46.56	21.02	1.07	1.12
Neil Mulholland	39	153	25.49%	58.72	15.66	38.26	1.76	1.44
Paul Nicholls	33	88	37.50%	68.26	5.40	45.87	2.07	2.12
Anthony Honeyball	28	84	33.33%	68.15	34.67	45.14	2.32	2.01
Colin Tizzard	21	109	19.27%	59.92	-26.43	31.68	1.43	1.67
Charlie Longsdon	19	89	21.35%	59.25	-13.01	34.54	1.71	1.64
Dan Skelton	17	76	22.37%	60.22	-6.53	33.38	1.51	1.63
Alan King	17	62	27.42%	64.61	-9.53	43.50	2.06	2.32
Dr Richard Newland	13	36	36.11%	63.80	6.20	41.67	2.52	2.48

HAYDOCK PARK

Trainer	Wins	Runs	Strike Rate	% Rivals Beaten	P/L	Run To Form %	Impact Value	Market Value
Donald McCain	19	101	18.81%	52.83	-10.41	30.83	1.40	1.11
Nigel Twiston-Davies	18	100	18.00%	58.50	-18.33	32.22	1.53	1.36
Venetia Williams	17	89	19.10%	51.30	75.25	25.84	1.61	1.34
Paul Nicholls	16	76	21.05%	60.16	-21.87	26.85	1.54	1.70
Sue Smith	13	119	10.92%	57.55	7.53	27.50	0.85	1.23
David Pipe	13	72	18.06%	57.56	63.00	26.39	1.81	1.38
Evan Williams	9	70	12.86%	49.61	34.00	23.24	1.03	1.14
Nicky Henderson	9	48	18.75%	58.24	-17.81	28.62	1.36	1.78
Lucinda Russell	9	72	12.50%	43.07	23.83	15.28	1.07	0.87
Jonjo O'Neill	8	64	12.50%	41.67	-11.77	14.06	1.14	1.29

HEREFORD

Trainer	Wins	Runs	Strike Rate	% Rivals Beaten	P/L	Run To Form %	Impact Value	Market Value
Venetia Williams	8	40	20.00%	43.05	8.23	22.50	1.61	1.24
Warren Greatrex	5	17	29.41%	76.33	-1.17	59.80	2.46	2.34
Henry Oliver	5	18	27.78%	60.23	25.50	46.15	2.49	1.21
Philip Hobbs	4	20	20.00%	66.03	-7.73	33.33	1.50	2.50
Dan Skelton	4	20	20.00%	50.98	-4.23	33.33	1.78	2.01
Nigel Twiston-Davies	4	24	16.67%	54.72	-8.75	21.87	1.27	1.65
David Rees	3	9	33.33%	55.39	9.88	42.86	3.07	1.20
Kerry Lee	3	32	9.38%	57.38	-16.25	19.27	0.71	1.24
Harry Fry	3	8	37.50%	68.56	4.45	71.43	2.63	2.70
Alex Hales	3	6	50.00%	72.16	9.75	58.33	3.20	0.80

HEXHAM

Trainer	Wins	Runs	Strike Rate	% Rivals Beaten	P/L	Run To Form %	Impact Value	Market Value
Lucinda Russell	41	244	16.80%	54.29	32.34	25.51	1.36	1.34
Maurice Barnes	18	118	15.25%	57.06	-11.38	30.97	1.33	1.14
Donald McCain	15	113	13.27%	51.91	-66.88	19.01	0.97	1.73
Micky Hammond	15	127	11.81%	51.71	-56.68	18.59	1.04	1.26
Stuart Coltherd	14	74	18.92%	57.26	27.50	29.41	1.68	1.43
Sue Smith	14	126	11.11%	57.88	-57.58	24.57	0.96	1.25
Nicky Richards	13	46	28.26%	60.25	15.31	36.96	2.48	1.83
James Ewart	11	57	19.30%	55.07	1.13	26.89	1.75	1.38
Brian Ellison	11	60	18.33%	58.76	-2.46	28.76	1.47	1.69
Martin Todhunter	11	90	12.22%	51.40	-19.38	21.11	1.01	1.13

HUNTINGDON

Trainer	Wins	Runs	Strike Rate	% Rivals Beaten	P/L	Run To Form %	Impact Value	Market Value
Nicky Henderson	31	96	32.29%	69.06	-12.34	44.43	2.48	2.52
Jonjo O'Neill	29	122	23.77%	57.90	11.04	32.08	1.97	1.58
Alan King	23	113	20.35%	65.57	-29.85	37.44	1.55	2.28
Kim Bailey	20	97	20.62%	56.20	29.98	37.77	1.71	1.35
Dan Skelton	20	125	16.00%	58.14	-42.38	30.91	1.23	1.65
Gary Moore	17	107	15.89%	50.95	32.71	27.10	1.24	1.25
Charlie Longsdon	17	100	17.00%	51.00	-12.90	33.34	1.29	1.42
Ben Pauling	11	54	20.37%	55.84	86.42	26.88	1.86	1.64
David Dennis	11	42	26.19%	63.17	30.46	35.71	2.04	1.35
Ian Williams	10	64	15.63%	52.96	-15.25	24.12	1.34	1.21

KELSO

Trainer	Wins	Runs	Strike Rate	% Rivals Beaten	P/L	Run To Form %	Impact Value	Market Value
Lucinda Russell	36	278	12.95%	54.37	-76.45	22.72	1.06	1.22
Donald McCain	36	167	21.56%	57.01	-2.04	29.04	1.63	1.77
N. W. Alexander	26	197	13.20%	48.94	39.08	20.00	1.10	0.97
Nicky Richards	26	134	19.40%	57.56	-17.81	26.85	1.52	1.75
James Ewart	17	106	16.04%	52.63	34.46	24.88	1.34	1.28
Rose Dobbin	16	142	11.27%	53.56	-11.06	21.16	1.04	1.19
Sandy Thomson	11	94	11.70%	57.29	33.58	26.99	1.00	1.20
Chris Grant	10	76	13.16%	49.23	79.60	23.83	1.10	0.88
Iain Jardine	9	51	17.65%	50.14	7.05	25.06	1.46	1.23
Dianne Sayer	8	92	8.70%	49.69	-38.00	17.79	0.73	1.07

KEMPTON PARK

Trainer	Wins	Runs	Strike Rate	% Rivals Beaten	P/L	Run To Form %	Impact Value	Market Value
Nicky Henderson	70	253	27.67%	62.95	-5.31	37.21	2.13	2.28
Paul Nicholls	43	206	20.87%	62.70	-26.69	34.56	1.51	1.77
Alan King	28	185	15.14%	54.96	-76.27	27.42	1.27	1.61
Harry Fry	19	74	25.68%	61.35	36.95	33.75	2.27	1.89
Nigel Twiston-Davies	12	70	17.14%	54.94	-24.39	20.30	1.43	1.31
Chris Gordon	12	64	18.75%	58.32	47.43	23.44	1.66	1.13
Jonjo O'Neill	12	109	11.01%	51.11	-49.89	20.67	1.00	1.30
Colin Tizzard	12	81	14.81%	56.02	18.98	23.67	1.22	1.12
Philip Hobbs	10	106	9.43%	53.81	-70.66	17.61	0.80	1.44
Emma Lavelle	10	77	12.99%	50.94	-28.27	30.64	1.07	1.40

LEICESTER

Trainer	Wins	Runs	Strike Rate	% Rivals Beaten	P/L	Run To Form %	Impact Value	Market Value
Nigel Twiston-Davies	18	67	26.87%	59.83	39.46	34.33	1.85	1.27
Tom George	16	50	32.00%	68.10	19.25	50.04	2.24	1.63
David Pipe	11	28	39.29%	65.71	11.06	42.86	2.38	2.12
Caroline Bailey	11	43	25.58%	57.95	1.49	33.38	1.78	1.20
Fergal O'Brien	8	43	18.60%	55.91	23.63	36.58	1.33	1.37
Venetia Williams	8	43	18.60%	57.53	-19.38	21.37	1.17	1.72
Robin Dickin	7	28	25.00%	53.34	11.63	39.29	1.61	1.21
Philip Hobbs	7	19	36.84%	71.08	3.58	47.46	2.63	2.52
Dan Skelton	6	30	20.00%	61.69	-2.28	24.44	1.38	1.53
Ian Williams	6	21	28.57%	57.82	-3.43	39.68	2.40	1.71

LINGFIELD PARK

Trainer	Wins	Runs	Strike Rate	% Rivals Beaten	P/L	Run To Form %	Impact Value	Market Value
Gary Moore	12	100	12.00%	47.54	-32.50	24.27	0.86	1.24
Warren Greatrex	11	27	40.74%	63.12	0.48	51.85	2.73	2.38
Seamus Mullins	9	54	16.67%	50.69	41.25	20.37	1.24	0.86
Nigel Twiston-Davies	8	28	28.57%	60.06	23.58	35.71	2.02	1.53
Nicky Henderson	8	22	36.36%	76.94	-0.58	63.16	2.44	2.73
Chris Gordon	8	44	18.18%	58.23	-14.15	32.53	1.21	1.24
Dan Skelton	6	17	35.29%	69.57	11.25	39.41	2.38	1.92
Dr Richard Newland	4	8	50.00%	74.06	1.95	70.00	3.59	2.79
Ali Stronge	4	9	44.44%	69.66	7.32	44.44	2.83	1.33
Emma Lavelle	4	19	21.05%	64.03	2.00	37.72	1.71	1.66

LUDLOW

Trainer	Wins	Runs	Strike Rate	% Rivals Beaten	P/L	Run To Form %	Impact Value	Market Value
Evan Williams	38	238	15.97%	53.11	-50.71	30.45	1.23	1.33
Nicky Henderson	29	102	28.43%	66.06	-20.86	40.27	2.47	2.81
Philip Hobbs	25	114	21.93%	62.32	-24.25	37.81	1.83	2.21
Henry Daly	23	112	20.54%	65.30	-15.02	33.77	1.69	1.47
Dan Skelton	22	107	20.56%	62.09	-20.08	32.75	1.76	1.91
Kim Bailey	20	108	18.52%	58.01	0.97	34.93	1.56	1.42
Nigel Twiston-Davies	18	148	12.16%	56.07	-79.22	24.74	1.01	1.49
Tom George	17	88	19.32%	65.48	-14.00	31.63	1.70	1.46
Venetia Williams	14	139	10.07%	53.37	-70.28	21.32	0.86	1.27
Ian Williams	13	65	20.00%	56.34	-4.41	31.24	1.69	1.48

TRAINERS FOR COURSES

MARKET RASEN

Trainer	Wins	Runs	Strike Rate	% Rivals Beaten	P/L	Run To Form %	Impact Value	Market Value
Dan Skelton	41	145	28.28%	64.08	26.23	36.00	2.11	1.90
Jonjo O'Neill	35	226	15.49%	51.40	-68.81	23.73	1.19	1.44
Charlie Longsdon	27	143	18.88%	58.51	-47.68	34.16	1.47	1.62
Brian Ellison	25	152	16.45%	49.36	-22.42	26.51	1.25	1.30
Nicky Henderson	24	76	31.58%	65.88	5.08	37.52	2.36	2.33
Fergal O'Brien	20	88	22.73%	55.61	49.13	34.60	1.68	1.25
Dr Richard Newland	19	74	25.68%	63.43	23.37	32.30	2.14	2.17
Peter Bowen	18	88	20.45%	58.14	-17.41	30.28	1.67	1.63
David Pipe	11	57	19.30%	54.51	-19.60	30.95	1.53	1.76
Nigel Hawke	11	46	23.91%	51.50	21.83	31.52	1.71	1.14

MUSSELBURGH

Trainer	Wins	Runs	Strike Rate	% Rivals Beaten	P/L	Run To Form %	Impact Value	Market Value
Lucinda Russell	35	263	13.31%	50.65	-25.45	25.70	1.04	1.09
Donald McCain	31	141	21.99%	59.32	37.20	32.53	1.57	1.42
Sandy Thomson	17	72	23.61%	64.78	58.05	34.26	1.89	1.55
Keith Dalgleish	14	48	29.17%	60.81	6.09	40.43	2.13	1.66
James Ewart	13	84	15.48%	51.12	5.05	25.99	1.31	1.31
Paul Nicholls	10	29	34.48%	65.56	3.72	44.83	2.20	1.94
Rose Dobbin	9	74	12.16%	47.75	7.25	28.38	1.02	1.20
Jim Goldie	9	99	9.09%	46.07	-35.09	13.44	0.79	0.88
Dianne Sayer	8	66	12.12%	51.98	-3.25	24.62	0.97	0.81
Chris Grant	8	73	10.96%	53.39	-17.00	23.82	0.91	0.91

NEWBURY

Trainer	Wins	Runs	Strike Rate	% Rivals Beaten	P/L	Run To Form %	Impact Value	Market Value
Nicky Henderson	50	194	25.77%	61.04	-7.46	38.69	2.34	2.14
Paul Nicholls	26	168	15.48%	55.38	-33.86	31.12	1.16	1.54
Philip Hobbs	24	128	18.75%	58.90	53.97	31.05	1.60	1.63
Alan King	21	166	12.65%	62.10	-55.72	34.65	1.12	1.45
David Pipe	16	101	15.84%	51.78	-0.97	25.29	1.56	1.21
Colin Tizzard	15	86	17.44%	59.23	-9.55	31.86	1.47	1.27
Harry Fry	12	63	19.05%	64.18	-12.33	34.09	1.70	2.37
Warren Greatrex	11	70	15.71%	55.49	-16.00	26.46	1.41	1.31
Venetia Williams	10	87	11.49%	48.10	-21.63	20.02	0.97	1.21
Ben Pauling	9	45	20.00%	52.82	-10.14	29.66	1.73	1.45

NEWCASTLE

Trainer	Wins	Runs	Strike Rate	% Rivals Beaten	P/L	Run To Form %	Impact Value	Market Value
Sue Smith	21	120	17.50%	60.03	-28.19	28.59	1.35	1.58
Lucinda Russell	19	137	13.87%	51.27	-46.59	23.44	1.03	1.21
N. W. Alexander	16	111	14.41%	48.70	-21.93	25.45	1.12	1.03
Nicky Richards	13	64	20.31%	61.90	-8.23	35.45	1.58	1.99
Brian Ellison	13	66	19.70%	58.10	-20.99	33.78	1.38	1.57
Donald McCain	11	87	12.64%	55.34	-23.48	31.66	0.85	1.61
Keith Dalgleish	10	23	43.48%	62.89	27.88	47.83	3.31	1.50
Philip Kirby	9	48	18.75%	52.61	2.17	28.26	1.54	0.98
Sandy Thomson	8	39	20.51%	57.81	2.53	26.59	1.51	1.54
Micky Hammond	8	76	10.53%	46.19	-19.13	25.49	0.73	0.92

NEWTON ABBOT

Trainer	Wins	Runs	Strike Rate	% Rivals Beaten	P/L	Run To Form %	Impact Value	Market Value
Paul Nicholls	48	152	31.58%	65.90	-33.60	40.99	1.91	2.39
Philip Hobbs	33	157	21.02%	60.78	14.39	30.13	1.61	1.72
Martin Hill	19	129	14.73%	51.01	13.98	22.07	1.26	1.17
Evan Williams	18	122	14.75%	54.82	-39.11	24.37	1.02	1.23
Tim Vaughan	15	100	15.00%	50.44	-19.50	21.37	1.30	1.30
Jonjo O'Neill	15	89	16.85%	51.41	-33.88	25.98	1.39	1.60
Jimmy Frost	14	166	8.43%	45.84	-47.38	18.49	0.73	0.75
Colin Tizzard	13	125	10.40%	56.46	-55.00	21.99	0.79	1.43
Jeremy Scott	13	77	16.88%	60.96	16.00	21.08	1.46	1.27
David Pipe	13	145	8.97%	48.77	-91.16	16.41	0.78	1.33

PERTH

Trainer	Wins	Runs	Strike Rate	% Rivals Beaten	P/L	Run To Form %	Impact Value	Market Value
Gordon Elliott, Ireland	67	249	26.91%	65.16	-3.59	40.98	1.74	2.03
Lucinda Russell	32	380	8.42%	48.45	-125.09	19.43	0.62	1.03
Fergal O'Brien	23	79	29.11%	59.91	35.88	38.61	2.06	1.46
Donald McCain	23	118	19.49%	53.16	-10.99	31.63	1.25	1.44
Lisa Harrison	23	166	13.86%	51.57	-5.08	26.17	1.07	0.96
Nicky Richards	21	130	16.15%	55.78	4.29	31.55	1.33	1.30
Nigel Twiston-Davies	21	94	22.34%	60.55	-14.65	30.35	1.66	1.85
Stuart Crawford, Ireland	17	152	11.18%	50.16	-68.57	21.75	0.85	1.06
Tom George	15	70	21.43%	61.91	-7.93	40.50	1.50	1.93
David Pipe	13	24	54.17%	82.19	23.11	54.17	3.12	1.99

TRAINERS FOR COURSES

PLUMPTON

Trainer	Wins	Runs	Strike Rate	% Rivals Beaten	P/L	Run To Form %	Impact Value	Market Value
Gary Moore	46	253	18.18%	59.00	-33.52	29.28	1.34	1.56
Chris Gordon	24	157	15.29%	54.50	46.16	23.73	1.21	1.18
Alan King	18	50	36.00%	68.10	-7.03	42.03	2.54	2.60
Paul Henderson	17	70	24.29%	56.50	25.01	33.85	1.64	1.11
Suzy Smith	16	62	25.81%	62.49	81.38	37.63	2.23	1.25
David Pipe	15	55	27.27%	63.20	12.44	35.94	1.95	2.02
Anthony Honeyball	14	41	34.15%	68.61	9.14	49.07	2.44	1.83
Sheena West	13	94	13.83%	55.36	-7.08	27.71	1.14	1.07
David Bridgwater	13	68	19.12%	59.60	-21.84	28.78	1.37	1.41
Seamus Mullins	13	133	9.77%	47.55	-68.42	19.84	0.67	1.09

SANDOWN PARK

Trainer	Wins	Runs	Strike Rate	% Rivals Beaten	P/L	Run To Form %	Impact Value	Market Value
Nicky Henderson	43	152	28.29%	61.76	16.97	40.59	2.26	1.87
Paul Nicholls	27	193	13.99%	55.48	-34.94	28.20	1.04	1.36
Gary Moore	24	120	20.00%	47.41	71.32	24.60	1.43	1.01
Philip Hobbs	16	84	19.05%	59.51	1.98	30.73	1.65	1.52
Alan King	12	67	17.91%	54.21	3.71	25.37	1.44	1.44
Nigel Twiston-Davies	10	62	16.13%	50.81	41.66	20.97	1.51	1.29
Venetia Williams	9	99	9.09%	51.28	-57.50	22.22	0.77	1.18
Fergal O'Brien	9	24	37.50%	61.72	32.46	41.67	3.59	1.56
Charlie Longsdon	7	62	11.29%	54.63	15.25	22.91	1.10	1.13
David Pipe	7	60	11.67%	49.08	-30.54	23.90	1.13	1.47

SEDGEFIELD

Trainer	Wins	Runs	Strike Rate	% Rivals Beaten	P/L	Run To Form %	Impact Value	Market Value
Donald McCain	60	290	20.69%	56.63	-27.47	31.72	1.37	1.61
Micky Hammond	35	237	14.77%	47.15	-44.99	19.55	1.08	0.96
Brian Ellison	35	157	22.29%	59.83	-24.92	30.62	1.57	1.64
Sue Smith	26	203	12.81%	59.20	-66.65	30.23	0.95	1.38
Kenneth Slack	20	71	28.17%	63.38	30.58	33.43	2.18	1.68
Neil Mulholland	19	41	46.34%	64.75	19.57	48.78	2.86	1.99
Dan Skelton	16	54	29.63%	67.86	-3.60	37.39	1.99	2.22
Dianne Sayer	16	84	19.05%	51.74	24.75	23.81	1.52	1.07
Chris Grant	16	154	10.39%	49.19	-32.69	21.14	0.76	0.86
James Ewart	10	59	16.95%	58.47	0.25	30.19	1.28	1.31

SOUTHWELL

Trainer	Wins	Runs	Strike Rate	% Rivals Beaten	P/L	Run To Form %	Impact Value	Market Value
Jonjo O'Neill	28	174	16.09%	60.25	-38.20	26.14	1.30	1.62
Dan Skelton	25	129	19.38%	63.26	-35.28	36.65	1.46	1.97
Tom George	23	73	31.51%	72.07	8.08	48.00	2.39	2.17
Caroline Bailey	22	102	21.57%	59.57	45.60	32.07	1.65	1.31
Charlie Longsdon	19	97	19.59%	57.43	2.09	28.81	1.53	1.79
Nicky Henderson	15	58	25.86%	66.50	-18.65	50.00	1.77	2.50
Tim Vaughan	13	98	13.27%	51.22	-7.10	19.46	0.96	1.16
Neil Mulholland	12	86	13.95%	52.63	-9.21	25.32	1.12	1.39
Ben Pauling	12	41	29.27%	65.10	-4.65	43.41	2.37	1.85
Kim Bailey	12	61	19.67%	63.41	17.23	36.41	1.45	1.62

STRATFORD-ON-AVON

Trainer	Wins	Runs	Strike Rate	% Rivals Beaten	P/L	Run To Form %	Impact Value	Market Value
Warren Greatrex	25	69	36.23%	66.88	37.94	40.61	2.76	2.32
Dan Skelton	24	124	19.35%	61.20	-24.32	29.71	1.48	1.75
Philip Hobbs	20	76	26.32%	59.96	31.43	33.52	2.00	1.60
Tom George	15	58	25.86%	62.80	37.84	36.45	1.96	1.79
Jonjo O'Neill	15	109	13.76%	52.80	-16.81	24.20	1.16	1.42
Alan King	15	51	29.41%	74.95	13.98	42.02	2.35	1.94
Tim Vaughan	14	108	12.96%	51.22	-29.55	24.72	1.12	1.17
Peter Bowen	12	59	20.34%	63.60	4.67	37.79	1.67	1.70
Charlie Longsdon	11	64	17.19%	55.32	-14.07	31.73	1.48	1.62
Neil Mulholland	11	65	16.92%	57.22	8.68	23.82	1.28	1.33

TAUNTON

Trainer	Wins	Runs	Strike Rate	% Rivals Beaten	P/L	Run To Form %	Impact Value	Market Value
Paul Nicholls	58	191	30.37%	72.22	-9.98	46.67	2.23	2.53
Philip Hobbs	22	135	16.30%	61.74	-55.56	33.78	1.45	1.97
Harry Fry	22	86	25.58%	70.44	-12.31	50.48	2.30	2.47
Colin Tizzard	18	123	14.63%	54.93	-19.85	26.90	1.23	1.38
David Pipe	17	178	9.55%	51.03	-87.12	20.09	0.88	1.31
Nicky Henderson	13	39	33.33%	72.42	3.55	49.33	2.60	2.49
Evan Williams	13	105	12.38%	46.88	-30.92	21.62	1.03	1.13
Anthony Honeyball	11	58	18.97%	55.52	20.08	31.45	1.76	1.34
Jeremy Scott	11	58	18.97%	56.37	7.25	23.29	1.70	1.09
Dan Skelton	11	62	17.74%	50.27	-20.15	25.28	1.45	1.56

TRAINERS FOR COURSES

TOWCESTER

Trainer	Wins	Runs	Strike Rate	% Rivals Beaten	P/L	Run To Form %	Impact Value	Market Value
Kim Bailey	19	78	24.36%	60.48	6.47	30.26	2.06	1.87
Fergal O'Brien	16	68	23.53%	57.62	14.63	29.36	2.00	1.84
Nicky Henderson	15	42	35.71%	78.13	-1.65	48.61	2.95	3.25
Ben Pauling	15	53	28.30%	58.54	45.00	36.74	2.40	1.74
Henry Oliver	12	41	29.27%	63.20	25.30	33.27	2.21	1.60
Henry Daly	12	42	28.57%	64.24	42.60	32.52	2.25	1.39
Charlie Longsdon	11	61	18.03%	58.61	-22.67	30.21	1.35	1.35
Alan King	10	38	26.32%	74.91	2.70	40.13	2.48	2.86
Nigel Twiston-Davies	9	81	11.11%	53.48	-27.13	21.12	0.90	1.39
Martin Keighley	9	61	14.75%	52.06	-18.75	23.45	1.26	1.18

UTTOXETER

Trainer	Wins	Runs	Strike Rate	% Rivals Beaten	P/L	Run To Form %	Impact Value	Market Value
Jonjo O'Neill	36	280	12.86%	50.54	-88.69	22.19	1.15	1.62
Charlie Longsdon	28	124	22.58%	59.75	10.55	33.69	2.03	1.70
Nigel Twiston-Davies	27	160	16.88%	58.56	-14.42	26.92	1.52	1.58
Dan Skelton	25	109	22.94%	64.40	-13.77	35.40	1.94	1.98
David Pipe	24	144	16.67%	57.29	-5.73	25.23	1.50	1.67
Warren Greatrex	23	64	35.94%	66.33	31.84	48.80	3.02	1.90
Philip Hobbs	21	111	18.92%	58.92	-7.67	29.14	1.68	1.75
Nicky Henderson	21	69	30.43%	67.88	-12.95	39.00	2.41	2.59
Sue Smith	19	115	16.52%	54.01	38.79	24.97	1.34	1.17
Tim Vaughan	19	160	11.88%	49.18	-56.18	19.09	1.08	1.31

WARWICK

Trainer	Wins	Runs	Strike Rate	% Rivals Beaten	P/L	Run To Form %	Impact Value	Market Value
Alan King	32	134	23.88%	67.20	-45.36	36.51	2.12	2.34
Dan Skelton	30	154	19.48%	56.76	-42.17	32.50	1.55	1.79
Philip Hobbs	26	109	23.85%	63.72	-12.05	37.15	1.96	2.19
Nigel Twiston-Davies	23	152	15.13%	55.84	-50.00	23.00	1.22	1.33
Jonjo O'Neill	21	147	14.29%	50.89	4.65	22.83	1.36	1.19
Venetia Williams	17	98	17.35%	54.55	-12.07	23.65	1.36	1.32
Nicky Henderson	14	53	26.42%	63.83	-9.46	39.88	2.18	2.23
Paul Nicholls	13	49	26.53%	67.71	-10.16	40.12	1.65	1.82
Henry Daly	12	64	18.75%	55.90	-8.38	25.00	1.79	1.47
Charlie Longsdon	12	107	11.21%	52.77	-49.01	22.86	1.01	1.41

WETHERBY

Trainer	Wins	Runs	Strike Rate	% Rivals Beaten	P/L	Run To Form %	Impact Value	Market Value
Sue Smith	31	227	13.66%	51.64	-94.65	24.36	1.09	1.29
Dan Skelton	30	89	33.71%	68.40	10.65	46.21	2.50	2.07
Micky Hammond	26	261	9.96%	45.99	-2.92	17.06	0.87	0.80
Philip Kirby	20	143	13.99%	46.69	-15.57	21.55	1.29	0.98
Warren Greatrex	20	67	29.85%	66.28	11.32	36.19	2.28	2.42
Brian Ellison	16	114	14.04%	55.85	-13.83	21.81	1.18	1.37
Donald McCain	16	127	12.60%	49.03	-43.42	22.91	1.03	1.42
Jonjo O'Neill	16	84	19.05%	59.12	-20.02	30.95	1.57	1.64
Kim Bailey	13	36	36.11%	72.65	28.66	60.71	2.56	2.15
Lucinda Russell	11	106	10.38%	48.24	-24.63	18.48	0.86	1.12

WINCANTON

Trainer	Wins	Runs	Strike Rate	% Rivals Beaten	P/L	Run To Form %	Impact Value	Market Value
Paul Nicholls	90	271	33.21%	66.77	-8.69	46.35	2.28	2.49
Colin Tizzard	35	256	13.67%	55.22	-68.32	25.59	1.14	1.36
Philip Hobbs	24	175	13.71%	55.37	-31.00	27.16	1.15	1.63
Harry Fry	21	95	22.11%	63.35	-3.13	35.46	1.89	2.06
David Pipe	16	109	14.68%	52.65	-32.31	27.43	1.38	1.64
Emma Lavelle	14	74	18.92%	63.02	16.38	31.70	1.64	1.38
Venetia Williams	14	94	14.89%	56.30	-27.77	32.87	1.14	1.42
Neil Mulholland	13	149	8.72%	53.01	-63.65	25.99	0.66	1.13
Alan King	12	74	16.22%	60.22	-16.11	25.17	1.30	1.88
Jeremy Scott	11	116	9.48%	46.91	-43.38	15.96	0.74	0.89

WORCESTER

Trainer	Wins	Runs	Strike Rate	% Rivals Beaten	P/L	Run To Form %	Impact Value	Market Value
Jonjo O'Neill	58	293	19.80%	57.61	-40.38	30.10	1.61	1.67
Philip Hobbs	31	116	26.72%	64.19	34.14	32.80	2.09	1.87
Neil Mulholland	27	161	16.77%	55.52	-19.09	30.32	1.39	1.37
Nicky Henderson	25	78	32.05%	69.33	12.94	40.61	2.45	2.34
David Pipe	24	161	14.91%	54.12	-60.14	22.74	1.24	1.52
Dan Skelton	23	126	18.25%	59.60	-32.22	24.46	1.46	1.89
Dr Richard Newland	22	79	27.85%	69.24	-17.92	40.75	2.15	2.19
Peter Bowen	21	100	21.00%	63.01	11.63	34.88	1.87	1.86
Nigel Twiston-Davies	20	110	18.18%	56.63	2.53	28.51	1.55	1.47
Paul Nicholls	17	54	31.48%	65.52	-4.96	46.00	2.11	2.13

FOLLOW THE FLAGS!

Horses In Focus

Top-Rated

Sectional Timing

Good Course Form

Warning Horses

Jockey & Trainer Uplift

Hot Trainer Form

Cold Trainer Form

Explore the Interactive Guide

**Find out about the ratings, Flags and symbols.
Get form and analysis explained in detail.**

Visit bit.ly/TFRPGuide today

BET BETTER

RACE CARDS

PLAY SMARTER

INDEX

INDEX

Index To Photographers

Benatar (right) and Finian's Oscar jump the last together at Ascot	*Francesca Altoft*	7
Cyrname was a very smart novice chaser last season	*Bill Selwyn*	14
Global Citizen on his way to victory in the Dovecote Novices' Hurdle	*Francesca Altoft*	20
Lostintranslation offered plenty to work on over hurdles last season	*Bill Selwyn*	25
Mr Big Shot resumes winning ways at Aintree under a delighted Tom Scudamore	*Bill Selwyn*	29
Posh Trish looks set to go over hurdles this season	*Bill Selwyn*	33
Santini is expected to take high rank amongst the novice chasers this season	*George Selwyn*	38
Topofthegame (pink) stays on strongly to win at Sandown	*Bill Selwyn*	44
Blackbow (right) and Carefully Selected (middle) chase home Tornado Flyer at Punchestown	*Bill Selwyn*	49
Dortmund Park is one to keep onside as a novice chaser this season	*Caroline Norris*	52
Presenting Percy looks tailor-made for the Gold Cup	*Caroline Norris*	56
Nicky Henderson was crowned champion trainer in Britain for a fifth time in 2017/18	*George Selwyn*	61
Thomas Patrick won three of his four starts over fences last season	*Bill Selwyn*	72
Blow By Blow on his way to victory in the Martin Pipe	*Caroline Norris*	74
Native River (right) and Might Bite jump the last as one in the Gold Cup	*Caroline Norris*	108
Footpad was unbeaten in five starts over fences this season	*Bill Selwyn*	109
Buveur d'Air retains his Champion Hurdle crown in gritty fashion	*George Selwyn*	111